HOW TO SURVIVE IN
ANCIENT
GREECE

D1564404

For Richard and Danielle
with love

HOW TO SURVIVE IN ANCIENT GREECE

AN EXPAT'S GUIDE TO LIVING IN CLASSICAL ATHENS (490-323 BCE)

ROBERT GARLAND

PEN & SWORD
HISTORY

AN IMPRINT OF PEN & SWORD BOOKS LTD.
YORKSHIRE – PHILADELPHIA

First published in Great Britain in 2020 and reprinted in 2022 by
PEN AND SWORD HISTORY
An imprint of
Pen & Sword Books Ltd
Yorkshire – Philadelphia

ISBN 978 1 52675 470 7

A CIP catalogue record for this book is available from the British Library.

Typeset in Times New Roman 11.5/14 by
Aura Technology and Software Services, India.
Printed and bound in the UK by CPI Group (UK) Ltd, Croydon, CRO 4YY

Pen & Sword Books Limited incorporates the imprints of Atlas, Archaeology,
Aviation, Discovery, Family History, Fiction, History, Maritime, Military,
Military Classics, Politics, Select, Transport, True Crime, Air World, Frontline
Publishing, Leo Cooper, Remember When, Seaforth Publishing, The Praetorian
Press, Wharncliffe Local History, Wharncliffe Transport, Wharncliffe True Crime
and White Owl.

For a complete list of Pen & Sword titles please contact
PEN & SWORD BOOKS LIMITED
47 Church Street, Barnsley, South Yorkshire, S70 2AS, England
E-mail: enquiries@pen-and-sword.co.uk
Website: www.pen-and-sword.co.uk

Or

PEN AND SWORD BOOKS
1950 Lawrence Rd, Havertown, PA 19083, USA
E-mail: Uspen-and-sword@casematepublishers.com
Website: www.penandswordbooks.com

Contents

Contents

Acknowledgements

I wish to express my deep appreciation of the dear friends who have helped me to see the many ways in which history is inescapably present: Tony Aveni, Peter Balakian, Stan Brubaker, Paul Cartledge, Susan Dyer, Pat Easterling, Kiko Galvez, Mike Goldmark, Emma Greensmith, Graham Hodges, Sir Fergus Millar, Jon Mikalson, Alice and Sasha Nakhimovsky, John Naughton, Alan Swensen, David Whitehead, Robert Wilson, and as ever with gratitude to Sir Mick Jagger.

Introduction

How to Survive in Ancient Greece is not a history book in the conventional sense of the word. It's asking you to imagine that you suddenly find yourself transported back in time and place and discover a landscape for which you are completely unprepared. What do you need to know in order to survive? What will look vaguely familiar? What will seem radically different? What kind of people will you encounter? How will you expect them to interact with you – and you with them? What work will be available? How will you relax? What will you do if you become sick? How will you fit in? Can you fit in? That last decision, of course, is yours and yours alone. History at its best is always about imagining a past world. This book invites you to take an active role in bringing to life the world of Ancient Greece and placing yourself squarely within it.

The world you are going to enter is that of late-fifth century Athens. I've chosen this period because it was one of the greatest moments of human achievement and is very well documented. The year is 420 BCE, when Athens and Sparta are enjoying an uneasy peace. At the time you arrive Athens' manpower is getting back up to strength after a devastating plague, she rules a maritime empire that dominates the eastern Mediterranean, she has invested more faith in the judgement of the common man than any society before or since, Sophocles and Euripides are writing tragedies that will stir and provoke audiences 2,400 years later, medical science is advancing, Socrates is getting a lot of people's backs up by telling them they need to rid themselves of all their unexamined opinions, and the Parthenon, the greatest Greek temple ever built, crowns the Acropolis. In short, human excellence has reached a peak. You might not want to stay too long, however, for five years later Athens will take a decision that will set her on a downward spiral, ultimately leading to her total defeat at the hands of Sparta and her allies.

Since this isn't a conventional history book, I've taken one or two liberties with time in the interests of, well, interest. For instance, I've commandeered Aristotle as an occasional witness, even though he was born a generation later, both because I thought you'd want to hear from him and because what he says is representative of some widely held beliefs, not least regarding women.

I've tried to provide as much information about what to expect when you arrive, irrespective of your gender and age. It's fair to say, however, that if you're a female, you're going to have to make a bigger adjustment to life in ancient Greece than you will if you're a male.

Travelling back in time requires a big mental as well as physical adjustment, and I've done my best to prepare you for both. That's why I've included a number of interviews with Greeks from different walks of life and different places, hoping that these will help you to see the world from their perspective and further prepare you for what to expect.

Timeline

All dates are BCE unless otherwise indicated.

c.1200 The Trojan War takes place?

594-3 Solon, sometimes called the 'Father of Democracy', introduces constitutional, economic and social reforms in Athens.

508-507 Cleisthenes, also sometimes called the 'Father of Democracy', introduces administrative changes that lead Athens further down the road to democracy.

490 The Athenian infantry victory over the Persians at the Battle of Marathon conventionally marks the beginning of the Classical era.

483 The Athenians discover a rich vein of silver in Attica and on the recommendation of a leading politician called Themistocles begin building a large fleet with the proceeds.

480 The Persians under King Xerxes invade Greece. Some 300 Spartans, together with a force of helots, die opposing the Persians at Thermopylae in northern Greece. Mostly due to the Athenians, who contribute the largest number of ships, the Greek fleet defeats the Persians at the Battle of Salamis off the coast of Attica.

479 The Persians abandon their invasion after suffering a defeat at the hands of a combined Greek army at the Battle of Plataea in central Greece.

478 Greek states under the leadership of Athens form an alliance against Persia known as the Delian Confederacy, thereby laying the foundations for what will later become the Athenian Empire.

464 An earthquake in Sparta prompts its slaves, known as helots, to revolt.

461 A largely peaceful political revolution moves Athens towards radical democracy.

458 Aeschylus' trilogy, *Oresteia*, wins first prize at the Great Dionysia festival.

447	At the suggestion of Pericles, the Athenians pass a resolution to rebuild the temples on the Acropolis burned down by the Persians.
431	The Peloponnesian War, fought between the Athenians and their allies and the Spartans and their allies, breaks out. The Spartan king, Archidamus, undertakes a series of annual invasions of Attica.
430-29	Athens is ravaged by a plague, resulting in the evacuation of its rural population inside the city walls.
425	The Athenians capture 290 Spartans on the island of Sphacteria in the southern Peloponnese, thereby forcing the Spartans to abandon their annual invasions of Attica.
421	Athens and Sparta make peace.
415	Athens dispatches an expedition to conquer Sicily.
413	The Sicilian expedition is wiped out by the Syracusans and all the surviving Athenians are taken prisoner. Soon afterwards Sparta resumes hostilities against Athens.
404	Athens surrenders to Sparta, thereby ending the Peloponnesian War.
404-403	A Spartan-backed oligarchy known as the Thirty Tyrants rules Athens.
403	The Thirty Tyrants are expelled and Athenian democracy is restored.
399	Socrates is condemned to death by the restored democracy.
c. 385	Plato founds a school of philosophy in the Grove of Academus in Athens.
338	Philip II of Macedon defeats a coalition of Greek states led by Athens at the Battle of Chaeronea in central Greece. He acquires undisputed control of the Greek mainland.
336	The assassination of Philip II leads to the accession of his son, Alexander the Great.
334	Alexander crosses into modern-day Turkey to attack the Persian Empire.
331	Alexander founds Alexandria in Egypt.
323	The death of Alexander at Babylon leads to the fragmentation of his empire into three large blocs. This event conventionally marks the end of the Classical era.
322	Athens falls under Macedonian domination.

Things You Should Know

As an expat, you're going to be residing in Classical Athens. 'Classical' means the period from 490-323 BCE, from the Battle of Marathon, which the Athenians fight and win against the Persian invaders under King Xerxes, to the death of Alexander the Great, king of Macedon, by which time Athenian democracy has been sharply curtailed and Greek freedom has been virtually extinguished.

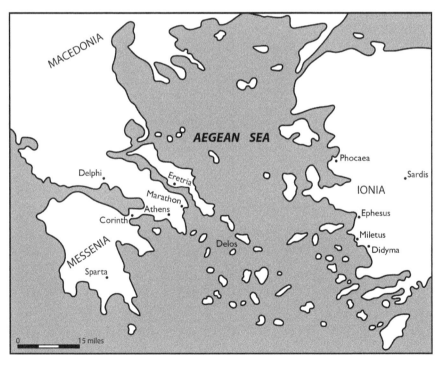

Map of Greece.

What makes Classical Athens so special?

Most of our evidence about Classical Greece comes from Athens, the city named after the goddess Athena. That's because the Athenians are both highly literate and very accomplished in all branches of artistic expression. This helps us to envisage how they lived in some detail.

We know much less about how, say, the Spartans lived. They have left few archaeological traces and no writings that describe what life was like in Sparta. Most of what we know about them is preserved in the writings of non-Spartans, the foremost of whom, a biographer and moralist called Plutarch, lived in the Roman period hundreds of years after Sparta's eclipse. We know next-to-nothing about the daily lives of those who reside in other Greek *poleis* or city-states – about one thousand in all – such as Corinth, Thebes, Syracuse, Mytilene, Miletus, and so forth, even though these *poleis* were very important.

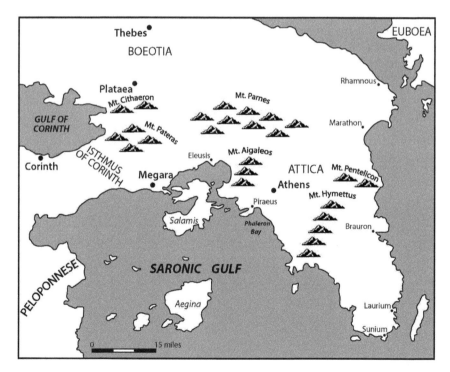

Map of Attica.

A *polis* consists of both territory and an urban centre. It is self-governing and largely self-sufficient. There are also a number of peoples on the Greek mainland who occupy territories that do not possess an urban centre. How they conduct their affairs and their daily lives is a complete mystery. They have left behind no visible traces of their existence.

Athens' surrounding landmass, known as Attica, is shaped like an elongated carrot and comprises some 1,000 square miles. It's about the size of Derbyshire, or Rhode Island, the smallest American state, if you happen to be American. Its urban centre is more like a medium-sized provincial town than a metropolis in our understanding of the word. Farm animals are a common sight in built-up areas, as they are throughout the ancient world. Passageways between houses are narrow and winding. Most roads consist of beaten earth. They are dusty in the summer and muddy in the winter.

The total population of Attica is about 150,000, half of whom live in Athens and the other half in the countryside. Approximately half of the population, too, are slaves and will remain so all their lives. This, therefore, is a very different kind of slavery from the one practised by the Romans, who regularly grant freedom to slaves after they have performed several years of faithful and devoted service.

Classical Athens is remarkable by any standards, having produced more men of genius *per capita* than any other place in history. Its contribution to western civilization – in literature, art, history, architecture, philosophy and many branches of science, including astronomy and medicine – is unparalleled. Athens reaches its peak in the mid- to late-430s, when new temples are rising on the Acropolis following the Persian conflagration and before the disastrous Peloponnesian War breaks out in 431. However, it briefly recovers fifteen years later, just before dispatching the doomed expedition to conquer Sicily.

What you should know about Athenian history

It's essential for you to know a bit about the two major events that happen in the fifth century so that you can converse knowledgeably with the Athenians you encounter. The first is the Graeco-Persian Wars. The Persians expected to win that battle and obliterate Athens from the face of the earth. They had a grudge against the city because it had given military assistance to Greeks living in Ionia – modern day western Turkey – who were rebelling against their empire. But they were defeated by a much smaller Athenian army. Marathon was like the Battle of Britain: it totally gripped the Athenian imagination and still does.

The Persians returned ten years later with a vast army led by King Xerxes. This time around they had it in mind to conquer the whole of Greece. They got as far as Athens, which they burned to the ground, but they were defeated at sea and, later, on land. Before the naval battle, the Athenians had evacuated their civilian population to the island of Salamis, barely a mile from the coast of Attica. Since the battle took place in the straits, the refugees had a front row view of the conflict. It must

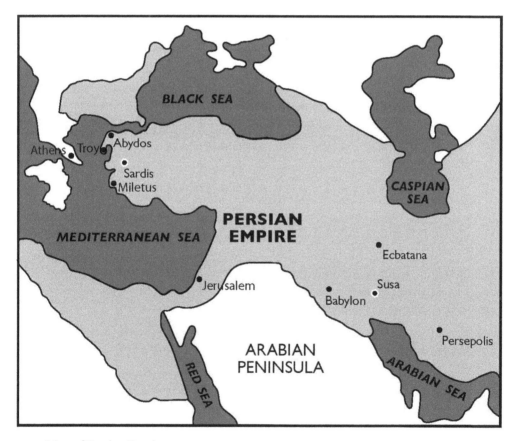

Map of Persian Empire.

have been an agonising moment. Had the Persians won, they would have landed on Salamis, killed all the men, and enslaved the women and children. I should point out that this treatment of the defeated was not uncommon in the ancient world, and though it was certainly barbaric, it was by no means exclusively 'barbarian'.

As you would expect, the Athenians hate the Persians for destroying their city, but don't assume that they hate them for being Persians. Though Greeks generally look down on non-Greeks and assume that their culture is superior, there's no convincing evidence that they're infected by our colour-based racism. You may meet Athenians who are good friends with Persians.

After the Persians had withdrawn from the Greek mainland, the Athenians became head of the Delian League; a maritime confederacy of about 150 Greek states, so-named because its headquarters were on the island of Delos in the centre of the Cyclades. The name 'Cyclades' means the 'circling islands' because they roughly form a circle. By the middle of the fifth century, following attempts by some states to secede, the Delian League had become an instrument of Athenian imperialism. Membership was no longer optional; it was forbidden to secede, and most of the so-called allies were required to pay an annual tribute, though a few privileged members contributed ships.

The other really big event is the Peloponnesian War, which was fought between Athens and Sparta and their respective allies. It broke out in 431 and will come to an end in 404, with a cessation in hostilities from 421 to 413. The Athenian historian Thucydides, who is writing a history of the war, comments that no campaign in history was more calamitous for the defeated than Athens' invasion of Sicily, which occurs during this interval. The naval expedition sets out with high hopes in 415 and suffers total defeat two years later. 'Out of many who left, few returned home,' Thucydides tersely reports; a characteristically Greek understatement. It is well worth reading Thucydides' history before you travel back to ancient Greece. He's the father of political science.

Immediately after their defeat in Sicily, the Athenians find themselves fighting for their lives. The city holds outs – against all odds – for nearly ten years, but is ultimately starved into submission. Its walls are destroyed and it is deprived of all but twelve ships. Though its glory days are over, it is not, however, destroyed.

The Peloponnesian War will prove a watershed in Greek history. Though Athens will recover remarkably quickly after the defeat, and even head a new alliance, the city will never be the same again. There is an irony to this, which is that her democratic institutions will become more effective in response to the mistakes that she made in the conduct of the Peloponnesian War.

The Spartans are the polar opposite of the Athenians. Whereas the Athenians are innovative, outward-going, enterprising, and cosmopolitan, the Spartans are inward-looking, conservative, unadventurous, and mistrustful of foreigners. The two societies perfectly exemplify the difference between what the French anthropologist Claude Lévi-Strauss identified as hot and cold societies, Athens being virtually at boiling point and Sparta being freezing cold. Sparta's conservatism is not a modern mirage. The inability to change and adapt will lead to her gradual demise in the fourth century, just as Athens' risk-taking mentality will lead to a more sudden downfall. It's regrettable the two sides never learn from each other. We rarely have the humility to learn from our enemies.

What Athens looks like

Athens is a walled city, pierced with numerous gates. The wall in question was built at the instigation of the politician and general Themistocles, following the departure of the Persian invaders in 480. It utilises the remains of the temples, statues and grave monuments that the Persians destroyed after the Athenians had evacuated the city. Athens is also protected by the so-called Long Walls, some 200m apart, which join it to its coastal city called the Piraeus, which is the second largest city in Attica. At the time you arrive, the Piraeus is the foremost trading port in the Classical world and the home of Athens' formidable fleet. It possesses three harbours, the largest of which, known as the Goblet, because of its shape, also handles exports and imports.

The Greeks take enormous pride in their public buildings, and this is especially true of the Athenians. This point is strikingly demonstrated by the spectacular temples that adorn the city, particularly those on the Acropolis. 'Acropolis' means literally 'high part of the city'. It denotes the imposing rock with an artificially levelled platform, roughly rectangular in shape, which still dominates the skyline of the Greek capital today.

Of these temples, none is more eye-catching than the Parthenon, meaning the 'temple of the Maiden'; the maiden in question being Athens' foremost deity, Athena. The Parthenon is a stunning testimony to Athens'

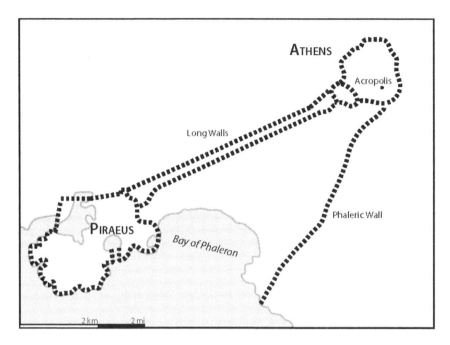

Map of Piraeus.

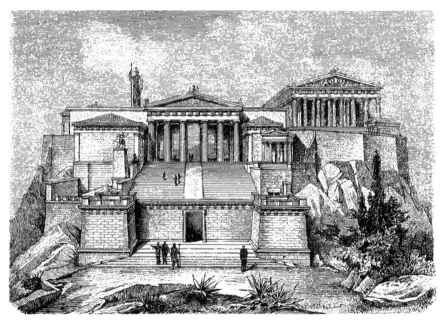

The Acropolis.

The Parthenon.

unique standing in the Greek-speaking world, as both cultural leader and imperial powerhouse. Housed within it is a gigantic resplendent image of the goddess, 12m high and covered in gold and silver over a sculpted wooden core. Other spectacular buildings adorn the Acropolis, including a monumental entrance gateway known as the Propylaea.

In stark contrast to this public magnificence, there are few signs of private wealth, even though some Athenians, as in any society, are very wealthy. But even the wealthy live frugally by modern standards. The visitor will therefore be struck by the rundown appearance of private dwellings, compared with the opulence and scale of the public buildings. What compensates for this disparity is the sense of civic pride, which is unlike anything that we understand or are capable of emulating today. When the Athenians experience a financial windfall in 483 as a result of the discovery of a rich vein of silver at Laurium in south Attica, they use it to construct a fleet, instead of giving themselves a general handout – or a tax cut – as we might do today. Later, they spend the surplus of the tribute that the 'allies' pay to their coffers to rebuild what the Persians destroyed on the Acropolis.

What life is like in the city

The centre of any *polis* is an open space known as the *agora*, which constitutes the civic, legal and commercial heart of the community.

The Athenian Agora (capital 'a' in this one case) lies to the north of the Acropolis. Males have to be at least eighteen to enter. Women are discouraged from entering, unless they are retailers. The most common type of building in any *agora* is the *stoa*, a structure with a colonnaded front, which provides shelter from the sun in the summer and from the wind, rain and occasional snow in winter. It is here that men make business deals. For that reason, bankers set up their tables inside *stoas*. The word for 'bank' in both ancient and modern Greek is *trapeza*, meaning 'table'.

The Agora also houses the law courts. Cases are held in the open in several designated areas. The juries are very large – some as large as 601 – the intention being to prevent bribery. The Athenians are very litigious and their courts sit for about 200 days a year; virtually all the days when they aren't celebrating state-funded festivals.

On the west side of the Agora is a row of life-size bronze statues standing on a plinth. These represent the ten eponymous heroes, who gave their names to the ten Athenian tribes into which the citizen body is divided. Attached to the plinth is a notice board where all public business is announced. Close by is a circular building known as the Tholos, where fifty members of the Council of 500 from one of the ten tribes are fed at public expense while they deliberate. Seventeen of these fifty members spend the night in the Tholos so that they are on hand 24/7 to deal with any emergency that might arise. It is the duty of the Council to prepare the agenda for meetings of the Assembly. The Council also debates all the issues in advance of each meeting in order to determine which of them will carry their recommendation.

There are many other civic buildings in the Athenian Agora, as well as a number of temples and religious structures. On the hill on the west side of the Agora is the Temple of Hephaestus, located in a district where metalworkers ply their trade under the patronage of their god.
The Agora is the commercial centre of Athens, attracting merchants from all over the Aegean. At dawn retailers set up temporary stalls where agricultural products and manufactured goods can be purchased.

Finally, an *agora* is a place to chat and exchange gossip, as suggested by the verb *agorazein*, which, among other meanings, approximates to 'loaf about in the agora'. Groups with similar interests or backgrounds, as well as foreigners hailing from the same city, have their favourite meeting places. Philosophers, such as the Stoics, whose name derives from the painted *stoa* in which they gather daily, will gather here about 150 years later to debate the nature of virtue and other topics.

How the city is run

The citizen body consists of between 30,000 to 50,000 freeborn males whose parents are both freeborn Athenian. They are known as the *Dêmos*, which means the 'People'. The People enjoy absolute power because Athens is a radical, or direct, democracy. There is no government and opposition, no political parties, no prime minister or president, and no elections. Every important decision pertaining to the state is decided by a vote of the People in the Assembly. In other words, every vote is a referendum. All citizens enjoy equality before the law and, if charged with any crime, they are judged by a jury of their peers.

Service in the military is required of all citizens. The cavalry plays a very limited role in Greek warfare, owing to the unevenness of the terrain. Those who can afford to purchase a suit of armour – helmet, greaves, breastplate, sword and spear – serve as heavily-armed infantry known as hoplites. The word 'hoplite' comes from the Greek word *hoplon,* the large round shield carried by a hoplite, which is his most distinctive piece of equipment. Those unable to afford a suit of armour are required to serve as rowers in the fleet. All citizens are called upon to serve on a rotating basis, the military being divided into the ten tribes that are used for all administrative purposes. In Sparta, by contrast, Athens' bugbear, the citizen body is perpetually under arms.

As indicated, Athens is a very open city that welcomes foreigners, both as visitors and as residents. It hosts perhaps as many as 20,000 so-called 'metics', foreigners who reside within its borders. This makes it unique in the Greek-speaking world. Most metics live in the Piraeus and are engaged in trade. The vast majority are citizens of other Greek *poleis*, but a few are non-Greeks, including Phoenicians and Egyptians. Their talents contribute significantly to the vitality of Athenian culture and many have become very prosperous. As a sign of their importance and inclusion, they are permitted to participate in the Panathenaea, Athens' premier festival. In time of war they serve in the army or navy, but they are also free to leave Athens and return to their homelands if they choose.

10

How religion works

The Greeks are polytheists. Zeus, the so-called 'father of gods and men', who wields the lightning bolt, is the most powerful, but he's anything but omnipotent, since his fellow Olympian deities, who constitute a fractious and highly dysfunctional family, also exercise considerable power. The Olympians are so-named because they live on Mount Olympus in the Pindus range in northern Greece. Mountaineering is not a sport in the ancient world, so no Greek has ever climbed to the summit of Mount Olympus to discover that there are no gods living up on top.

Zeus with his eagle seated on his throne. Coin minted in the name of Alexander the Great.

The majority of gods who are worshipped throughout the Greek-speaking world are variants of the Olympian deities and were already known to Homer. They include: Zeus, god of oaths and hospitality; Hera, goddess of marriage; Poseidon, god of the sea; Hades, god of the Underworld; Athena, goddess of female arts and war; Ares, god of war; Hermes, messenger of the gods and god of commerce; Demeter, goddess of the corn and the harvest; Dionysus, god of wine and the theatre; Aphrodite, goddess of love and beauty; Artemis, goddess of hunting and protector of wild beasts; Apollo, god of music, healing and prophecy; and Hephaestus, lame god of metalworking. Each of these gods has other areas under her or his control, but these are their main responsibilities.

In addition, they all have second names, so to speak, depending on where they are worshipped or which characteristic is being attributed to them. On the Athenian Acropolis alone, four separate Athenas are worshipped: Athena Parthenos (Maiden), Athena Polias (Of the city), Athena Promachos (She who fights in the front rank), and Athena Hygieia (Health). The Athenians don't have exclusive entitlement to

Athena wearing helmet.

Athena's goodwill, however. For instance, the Spartans venerate Athena Poliouchos (Guardian of the city) as one of their foremost deities, along with variations of all the other Olympian deities. When Greeks go to war, therefore, both sides regularly evoke the same gods, albeit by a different cult title.

Observance is conducted in the open around an altar. Temples merely house the cult-statue and offerings to the gods. The Parthenon has been aptly likened to an ornate jewellery box, its primary function being to give pleasure to Athena and to provide her with a 'residence' when she visits the city.

The gods are anthropomorphic, i.e. they resemble human beings both physically and in their psychological makeup. This is why they take pleasure in the smell of the roasting animals that are sacrificed in their honour. They also enjoy watching humans displaying their prowess at athletic, equestrian and musical contests, and for this reason these events are regularly incorporated into their festivals.

The priesthood is not a vocation and priests are not in the business of offering spiritual assistance or counsel to worshippers. Be warned: there are no therapists in ancient Greece. The main function of priests and priestesses is to oversee the sanctuary under their control and to supervise the observances that are conducted within it. They are not expected to set an example, moral or otherwise, in large part because Greek religion does not promote morality. Piety towards the gods and the dead, not good behaviour, is its central aim. The Greeks invoke their gods to do harm to their enemies just as frequently as they invoke them to give benefits to themselves or their family.

Priests serve gods and priestesses serve goddesses. Some priesthoods are open to every citizen, depending only on gender, others are hereditary in specific kin-groups, and still others are open to anyone who pays the requisite fee for the privilege. Most priests hold office for only a year, but some serve for life. In Athens, the most important priesthood is that of Athena Polias (Of the city). Her priestess is appointed from the ranks of one of Athens' most venerable kin-groups, the Eteoboutadai. She has no political influence, however, because as a woman she cannot attend the Assembly. So far as we know, priests never constituted a political lobby or interest group. In fact the opposite is likely to have been the case, since they have to compete with one another for state funding. The Eteoboutadai also supply the priest of the second most important cult in Athens, that of Poseidon Erechtheus. Erechtheus is the name of an early king of Athens, whose name became attached to Poseidon only in relation to this one cult.

The worship of the Olympians is only one aspect of Greek religion, however. Another important group are the chthonic deities, whose name derives from *chôn* meaning 'earth', since they live underground. We know much less about chthonic deities than we do about the Olympians because temples are not built in their honour and festivals are not celebrated in their name. But though they do not command the same resources as the Olympians, they are still very powerful.

The best place to become acquainted with their *modus operandi* is in the final play of Aeschylus' trilogy *Oresteia,* which is entitled *Eumenides* or 'Kindly Ones'; a euphemism for a particularly vengeful group of chthonic deities known as the Furies. As soon as Orestes murders his mother to avenge his father, the Furies pursue him relentlessly. Aeschylus suggests they are vile and repellent women with snakes in their hair and rasping breath. At the end of the play, however, they are transformed into the Kindly Ones, the title of the play, and offered an honoured place in the state with a cult on the north flank of the Acropolis.

A third important aspect of Greek religion is hero worship. The word 'hero' in this context means something very different from its English

Alexander the Great wearing skin of the Nemean lion. Coin minted in the name of Alexander the Great.

14

usage. It refers to a person whose life has been exceptional, whether for good or ill. The most celebrated hero is Herakles, Roman name Hercules, who, among his twelve labours, slew the Nemean lion. To demonstrate his descent from Herakles, Alexander the Great is depicted on coins wearing the lionskin. Another famous hero is Oedipus, who unknowingly killed his father and married his mother. His life is a testimony to the terrible consequences of mistaken identity and of the frightening power of coincidence. Heroes are powerful in the vicinity of their graves and can be summoned to help the city-state in which their bones reside in times of crisis. The way to restore their vitality and enlist their support is by offering them a blood sacrifice at their graves. The blood restores their vigour.

I've talked about the gods at some length because you're going to have to deal with them a lot. You'll probably arrive by sea, not least because the Greeks are a seafaring nation. I don't want to alarm you but make sure you sacrifice to Poseidon before boarding. Homer's *Odyssey* constantly emphasises the dangerous hazards of the deep, since weather conditions in the Aegean Sea are highly unpredictable and storms often arise without warning. The implacable enmity of Poseidon to Odysseus is therefore based on a frightening reality. Ostensibly that enmity is caused by Odysseus' blinding of Poseidon's one-eyed son, the giant Polyphemus, but all Greek mariners know that the sea god is to be greatly feared.

What the 'family' means in ancient Greece

The Greeks, who proverbially have a word for everything, do not have a word for 'family'. The nearest equivalent is *oikos* or *oikia*, more accurately translated as 'household'. Both words refer equally to a group of people living under the same roof and to the property that their household owns; namely the house and its outbuildings, the land upon which it stands, and all its household effects, including slaves. In short, the *oikos* is both people and property.

Husbands are typically at least ten years older than their wives. Many girls marry at the onset of puberty or shortly afterwards, the belief being that this will maximize their child-rearing capacity. In reality this practice has the very opposite effect, since many young girls are biologically ill-equipped to give birth shortly after puberty and become permanently damaged as a result. The frequency with which they become pregnant further debilitates them. As a result, the life expectancy of a woman is estimated to have been about ten years less than that of a man.

Well-to-do women are not permitted outside the home unattended. Unless accompanied by a family member, they must be escorted by a domestic slave. They are covered up from head to toe, with a headscarf and a veil sometimes drawn over the face. Lowborn women enjoy much more freedom, since many of them are forced to leave the house to perform regular daily tasks, such as fetching water from the local well.

It is the duty of every man to marry and perpetuate his *oikos*, and we'll be talking later about what being married meant for both the husband and the wife. You may have the view that all Greek males are homosexual, and I want to correct that common misperception. Although there is plenty of literary and pictorial evidence to indicate that the Greeks not only tolerate homosexuality but also advocate it in certain contexts, unlike in our society they regard it as an episodic phenomenon, viz. one that belongs to a particular period in life. In other words, it does not define a person's sexuality forever, so to speak. As a result, being what we call gay is frowned upon, largely because the Greeks put such a high premium on preserving the continuity of each individual household by producing a male heir or heirs.

And further on this topic, although the frequent depictions in Archaic (i.e. pre-Classical) art of the myth of Zeus' abduction of the beautiful youth Ganymede suggest a cultural acceptance of pederasty, it is certainly not tolerated in the period when you will be visiting. In Classical Athens sex with a minor is treated as a serious crime, punishable in some cases by death.

If you get sick or incapacitated, you'll have to rely on your family to look after you. There are only very limited means of support outside the family. A modest allowance is available to those who can prove disability status but pensions are unknown. The orphans of those who die in war are raised at public expense, but many others are forced to beg or are sold into slavery.

The majority of men and many women continue working until they become incapacitated. A minority are sufficiently wealthy to have a slave to look after them in old age.

How slavery functions

Most Athenians own at least one slave, whereas the wealthy own several. Slaves perform all manner of services for their masters and mistresses. It's important, however, to note that the institution embraces many different conditions and statuses. Those who work in the house are generally better treated than those who work outside in the fields. The worst off are those who toil in the silver mines and the marble quarries.

Abhorrent though the institution of slavery is, in the ancient world it affords to some individuals a degree of protection and security that is denied freeborn citizens at the bottom of the socio-economic heap. In Homer's *Odyssey,* when Odysseus meets Achilles in Hades and tries to console him for being dead by pointing out that he has left a great reputation behind him, Achilles retorts sharply that he would rather be a day labourer who works for another man than lord of all the dead. In other words, the worst condition he can imagine is working without job security and taking orders from someone else. This makes perfect sense once we bear in mind how dangerous and unpredictable life is in the ancient world, and that slaves receive regular sustenance and basic accommodation, whereas day labourers don't know where their next meal is coming from and must fend for themselves.

Another distinctive feature of Greek slavery is that, with the notable exception of the Spartan slave population known as helots, it is not racially based. Every Greek is at risk of becoming enslaved as a result of circumstance, chiefly by being captured in war. This means that Greeks cannot invariably tell whether a person is a slave merely by his or her physical appearance. That is a very important consideration to bear in mind as you walk around the streets of Athens.

No Greek to the best of our knowledge has ever questioned the fact that slavery is a part of the natural order of things. Aristotle goes so far as to claim that the deformities which slaves often experience as a result of the backbreaking work they perform is an indication that they are morally as well as anatomically inferior. He calls such persons 'slaves by nature', to distinguish them from those who have been born free but later for some reason become enslaved. There could be no more striking example of the mistaking of effect for cause. Aristotle also memorably described a household slave as 'property that breathes'. From his perspective, in other words, a slave is barely human. We don't know how widely shared this view was, but Aristotle certainly wasn't in a minority of one and it may well have been the norm rather than the exception.

What divides the wealthy from the poor?

Overwhelmingly our evidence about life in ancient Greece relates to the well-to-do, so we need to take a bold imaginative leap to envisage the lifestyle of the poor. A large percentage of the population of Athens are subsistence farmers with small holdings. A minority make money from their estates, which are worked by slaves, thereby enabling them to lead lives of complete leisure.

We also need to note that the tribute paid by Athens' allies to finance the fleet benefits the poor especially, since they serve as rowers and receive a daily wage for their service. It also supports the jury system, since jurors, too, receive a daily wage for their services. This is particularly beneficial to elderly citizens, who probably constitute the majority of the jury pool.

If you're well-to-do or wealthy, there are limited ways of spending money. The most essential item, almost equivalent to owning a car, is a slave. Horses are largely status symbols for the rich since they aren't much use except for riding short distances owing to the fact that Greece is very mountainous. A much-prized luxury item is high-class painted pottery, which is used at drinking parties. On its owner's decease, it is often deposited in his grave, which is why so much of it has survived in perfect condition.

Another luxury item is a prestigious funerary monument with sculpted figures. A wealthy family will pay a considerable sum of money to purchase a prime plot beside a well-frequented road. The most favoured burial area in Athens is the Potters' Quarter, known as the Ceramicus, situated on the west side of the city, just outside the city wall. Our word 'ceramic' derives in fact from Ceramicus. Today the area is a tranquil oasis amid the bustle of modern Athens. Tortoises sun themselves and frogs croak in the Eridanus River that runs through it, just as they did in the time of Socrates.

How to get around Athens

The only paved road inside Athens is the Panathenaic Way. This begins on the west side of the city at the Double Gate beside the Ceramicus and leads through the Agora up onto the Acropolis. It's not much more than half a mile in length. The most frequented road is the so-called Hamaxitos or Cart Road. The Hamaxitos follows the line of the Northern Long Wall and extends to the Piraeus, a distance of about five miles.

Types of amphoras.

Though it is unpaved, some sections of it are surfaced with broken stones. If a cart overturns or becomes stuck in the mud, however – a frequent occurrence – a traffic jam will be likely to ensue.

The usual way to transport supplies and products short distances is by employing a slave who bears a yoke on his back. The yoke is weighted down with an amphora, a two-handled vessel, looped to either end. Amphoras are the most common method of storing liquids, such as wine and olive oil, and solids, such as preserved fish and grains. They can be stacked on board a ship or in a cellar. An amphora has a knob at the bottom, which serves as a third handle when its contents are being poured out.

How to get rid of waste

You may have to hold your nose at times. You'll find large piles of refuse on every street corner, and the stench is often intolerable, especially in the summer months. A drain – which archaeologists have dubbed, rather grandiosely the Great Drain – runs through the Agora, but it is quite incapable of handling all the filth that is tossed into it, and, moreover, it regularly dries up in the summer months. In consequence, whenever it rains heavily, infected sewage runs through the streets.

Dung collectors periodically collect the refuse, which they are required to deposit at least half a mile from the city walls. It's the duty of publicly appointed officials to ensure that minimal standards of cleanliness are observed. However, though law enforcement officers known as *agoranomoi* prosecute defaulters, their number is hardly adequate to cope with the magnitude of the task. As a result, the disposal of waste is largely left up to the individual.

Because of the fear of pollution, thought of as an invisible contagion that spreads through the community much in the same way as a virus does, the dead cannot be buried inside the city walls. Pollution, known as *miasma*, is capable of being transmitted from one person to another by physical contact alone. In its most virulent form it can blight crops and cause pregnant women to miscarry. Belief in pollution may seem like a crackpot idea to you, but it does indicate a rudimentary awareness of the dangers of contagion. Mere contact with a corpse is believed to be a source of strong pollution, the 'remedy' for which is ritual purification. So this is just one more thing to be wary of.

What to do about crime

You won't be able to rely on the police if you get into a scrape. There's no police force, apart from a small contingent of publicly owned slaves from Scythia, a region that includes Eastern Europe and Central Asia. However, their job is to keep the peace, not to prevent or investigate crime, or indeed to catch criminals. Policing for the most part is done by those who live in the neighbourhood where the crime was committed; by ordinary citizens, in other words. This system is, nonetheless, surprisingly effective in detecting crime, though the method of dealing with apprehended felons tends to be somewhat rough and ready.

Fires are common, though there is no fire brigade, and earthquakes are a perennial hazard. There is no street lighting. I strongly advise you not to venture out at night unless accompanied by a slave bearing a torch to protect you.

What to do about germs

The answer is simple: you just have to forget about them. Sickness is common, especially in the summer in densely populated areas. This is largely because the Greeks have very little understanding of the importance of hygiene, with the result that their water supply is often contaminated. When Athens evacuates its rural population at the outset of the Peloponnesian War, thereby doubling the size of the city population, approximately one-third die as a result of an unidentified plague, possibly typhus, caused by the insanitary conditions.

A particularly melancholy fact is that deaths of mothers in childbirth are extremely common, as are neonatal deaths. Medea in Euripides' play of that name says she would rather fight in battle three times than give birth once. She knows whereof she speaks. Approximately one in three children die in the first year of their life – a grim statistic – largely due to diseases caused by poor sanitation.

Whereas we in the west today are experiencing a greying population, in Athens about half of the population is dead by the age of forty. As a result you'll encounter a much larger percentage of the population under the age of twenty than you will do of people over that age.

Other things to be aware of

Good news! There is the equivalent of a pub, though these often double up as brothels. There are no restaurants or fast food outlets. Meat is a luxury item, which only a small minority enjoy on a daily basis. If you're poor, you might eat meat only at public festivals, when hundreds of animals are slaughtered.

The seven-day week hasn't been invented and the calendar is lunar. As a result it's always falling out of alignment with the solar year. Festivals, liberally sprinkled throughout the year, form the same function as weekends do in our society.

Glass hasn't been invented, so windows are wide open in the day and boarded up at night. This makes life in the home uncomfortable in all weathers, since temperatures are very high in the summer and can be very low in winter (snow is not unknown).

There are no public toilets. Most people relieve themselves in the yard attached to their dwelling; if indeed they have a yard. If they're away from the house and get caught short, they relieve themselves in the bushes or in the street.

Very few houses have running water and none have indoor plumbing. Water is brought to the city by means of terracotta pipes from distant springs that feed public fountains. The pipes regularly leak at the joins and are often broken, resulting in an irregular or interrupted flow until the cause has been remedied. Pipes also feed the public fountains, which for the most part are simple stone basins cut into the living rock. Most families have to fetch water from wells or from fountains. This is an extremely arduous task and one that is often assigned to slaves.

How to survive without the Internet, email, or Twitter

I can't help you there. This is a slow-moving world as far as information and communication are concerned. We're used to news being reported almost the second it happens, but in ancient Greece it can take days or even longer to reach the outside world. This fact has a particular importance and poignancy in time of war. During the Sicilian Expedition, for instance, the Athenians will be wholly reliant for news of their army's progress on letters – what we might call communiqués – which Nicias, the senior general, writes – or more likely dictates – to a slave, and which, upon delivery, will be read out in the Assembly. And by the time that has happened, the situation on the ground will have changed dramatically. Aeschylus memorably noted that the only way the relatives of those serving overseas could find out whether their loved ones were alive or dead was by anxiously checking the dog tags attached to the cinerary urns that are periodically transported on board a trireme and unloaded on a quay in the Piraeus.

Plutarch tells us that the Athenians didn't learn of the disaster in Sicily until a stranger disembarked in the Piraeus. The stranger went to have his hair cut in a barber's shop and started talking about it as if it was common knowledge. The barber was gobsmacked – not too strong a word – so he downed his cutting instruments and belted five miles to Athens. When he arrived, he accosted some magistrates and related what he had heard. The magistrates immediately summoned an Assembly, at which the stranger was interrogated. Suspecting him of being the bearer of fake news, they charged him with disturbing the peace and fastened him to a wheel to torture him. Not long afterwards, however, messengers from Sicily arrived and confirmed the truth of his report.

Such is life in ancient Greece.

Introduction to Your New Home

What your house looks like

There aren't two distinct words for 'home' and 'house' in Greek. *Oikos* and *oikia* both mean 'house' and 'home'. As I pointed out earlier, this is further complicated by the fact that both *oikos* and *oikia* include the landed property, the livestock, the furniture, and the slaves. And as if all that isn't confusing enough, *oikos* and *oikia* are also the closest words to 'family' that exist in ancient Greek.

Most houses are flat-roofed dwellings made of mudbrick with a tiled roof. The mudbrick is often covered in plaster. There are two storeys at most. There's a door which may have a bolt, but thieves can always break in by burrowing through the walls. In the centre of the main room there's a hearth. There's no chimney; just a hole in the roof, by which the smoke, or at least some of it, escapes. Windows, if we can call them that, don't have glass panes. They only have shutters. This means that in cold weather, when the shutters are drawn across the windows, it's pretty dark and smoky. The only source of artificial lighting is provided by small lamps that burn animal fat. If you're well-to-do, you sleep in a wooden bed. If you're not, you sleep on the floor. This consists of beaten earth with perhaps matting or straw on top. You have few items of furniture; a couple of chairs, a stool or two, a small table, a chest, and perhaps some couches to recline and sleep on if you're really well-off. Bear in mind that wood is at a premium. A few objects hang from hooks around the walls, and there's a shelf for pottery.

In the courtyard there's a small altar made of mudbrick where you perform daily sacrifices to your household deities. If you're prosperous, you have a storehouse containing grain. Your farm animals wander very much at will. There are one or more flimsy structures a little distance from the house to accommodate your slaves, though your domestics sleep in the house. One of your slaves may be draining curds into a strainer with a cheesecloth, separating it from the yellowish whey. Another may be washing clothes in a barrel while one or two others are working your land.

The boundaries of your property are marked by a heap of stones. In some cases, these will take the form of herms; pillars mounted with the head of Hermes, god of boundaries as well as of commerce. The pillars are uncarved except for an erect penis. This is intended to be apotropaic. That's to say, it's intended to deter would-be malefactors and trespassers. Just before the Athenian expedition to Sicily sets sail, some vandals go around hacking off the penises and making gouges in the heads of the herms that are displayed on street corners throughout the city. It's suspected that their intention is for the act of desecration to be interpreted as a bad omen, which then results in the expedition being called off. If that *was* their intention, however, they failed. As you know by now, the expedition ends in total disaster two years later.

Women and the Family

How men regard women

Greek society is strongly patriarchal. There's no getting away from that – to us – highly unpalatable fact. But at least the Greeks don't think of women's bodies as dirty or polluted. There's no taboo on having sex with a menstruating woman and there's no need to purify yourself after having intercourse, as there is in some religions. Even so, some highly educated Greeks regard women's bodies to be inferior to those of men. Take what Aristotle wrote:

> A woman resembles an infertile male. She's female because of a kind of inadequacy. She can't use what she consumes to produce semen in its perfect form. This is due to the coldness of her nature.

Women's bodies, Aristotle explains, try to manufacture semen but they fail. Instead they produce menstrual discharge. This supposedly 'scientific' theory is, of course, based completely on prejudice. Anatomy as a science does not exist in Classical Greece, due to a strong religious taboo against dissecting the human body. I think it's a sure bet that most physicians never saw inside the body of a woman, whether she was dead or alive.

As further evidence of prejudice, I would point out that the father's role in conceiving a child is believed – by some at least – to be more important than that of the mother. Apollo describes the mother as 'merely the nurse of the newly sown seed' in Aeschylus' *Eumenides*, meaning a woman's womb is secondary to a father's sperm. With consummate lack of logic, however, Greek men invariably laid the failure to conceive at the door of the woman. Male sterility was beyond their ken.

There is also the deeply sexist belief that women are the originators of human misery. This is exemplified by the myth of Pandora; her name means 'All-gifted' or 'All-giving'. Zeus ordered Hephaestus, the god of the forge, to fashion Pandora out of clay to repay humans for the fact that the Titan Prometheus had given them fire. The woman was given the name Pandora because she had so many winning attributes. Zeus gave her a sealed jar and, being a woman, she was helplessly curious about its contents so couldn't refrain from opening it. As a result, hard labour, painful diseases and all the other evils that trouble humanity flew out into the world. Only hope remained inside the jar, and that explains why humans are incorrigibly hopeful.

The Greeks, or at least some of them, believed that women are incapable of controlling their lust. In Herodotus' history of the Graeco-Persian Wars, Gyges, the future king of Lydia declares, 'A woman removes her sense of shame when she removes her clothes.' This allegation may be partly based on the fact that Greek men have many 'legitimate' – i.e. socially acceptable – sexual outlets outside marriage, whereas Greek women have none and are required to remain faithful to their husbands. This double standard underpins the narrative in Homer's *Odyssey*. Whereas Odysseus swans around the Mediterranean – well, not quite as he does face several challenges and mishaps, but you get my point – sleeping with the nymph Calypso (seven years) and the witch Circe (one year), his poor old wife Penelope is left at home, having to fend off an army of suitors.

The kind of work that Greek women do

Before describing what kind of work Greek women perform, I need to provide you with some background about their status and lifestyle. These, as you'll soon discover, are very different from those enjoyed by women living in the west today.

To begin with, Greek women lead much more restricted and solitary lives. They can't vote, can't become jurors, can't (if they're respectable) appear in public unaccompanied, can't initiate a divorce or any other lawsuit, can't represent themselves in court, can't inherit in their own name, probably can't attend the theatre, and so on.

They have few opportunities for work. One occupation available to them is textile manufacture. Tapestry weaving in particular brings considerable honor and repute to women, though we need to note that this is performed in the home. I should also point out that arts and crafts aren't exclusively gender-specific. A vase in the red-figured style – that's to say, a vase that is decorated with figures painted in red against a black background – shows a female vase-painter decorating a mixing-bowl, and it's probably safe to assume that a minority of women find an outlet for their talents in other male-dominated crafts. It's often the fate of a woman who has been supported during her husband's lifetime to be forced to work for a living once she becomes a widow. Her chances of having to work therefore increase as she ages.

Some enterprising women work as 'female companions' or *hetairai*. These are the only women who are permitted to attend a drinking party, known as a symposium. We'll talk about symposia later. You shouldn't look down on women who choose this career path when you bump into them, as you surely will. Though some *hetairai* are hired for their sexual favours, it's one of the few professional outlets available to a freeborn woman. And it's also the case that *hetairai* are the only women who, as a group, are educated and politically informed. They need to be. It's almost part of the job description. That's because they mix in the very highest cultural, intellectual and political circles. As a result, some of them become extremely wealthy.

Women can also serve as priestesses and officiants, but we can hardly call that a career path, and, besides, such positions are only available to a select few. Another role for a woman is that of midwife, which I'll discuss later. You could also become a wet nurse, though most wet nurses are probably slaves.

How women have to behave

If you're a 'respectable' woman, you'll be expected to spend most of your time inside the home. It'll be your task to manage the running of the household, including the education of your children. Convention demands that you never leave your home unaccompanied. The statesman Pericles ended his famous speech on behalf of the war dead in the first year of the Peloponnesian War with the observation that 'a woman's greatest glory is to be talked about neither in praise nor in blame.' In

Woman dressed in
chitôn.

other words, you will be expected to be socially invisible. This is backed
up by a statement made by a female character in a play by Euripides:

> What's most scandalous is when a woman goes outdoors. I
> used to long to go out, but I stayed inside. I kept a lid on my
> mouth, unlike some women […] I didn't answer back to my
> husband and I gave him gentle looks. I knew when to get my
> way and when to let him get his way.

So she knows when to get her own way? Good to know that it's a two-
way street.

Modesty, however, is all important. When you do go outside, be
careful not to expose any part of your face or body. I suggest you drape
your cloak over your head to cover your face.

Very likely your husband will be out of the house most of the day, either working, engaged in public business, or merely chewing the cud in the Agora. He regards this as his male prerogative. He'll also spend many evenings at symposia, drinking with his mates and a few *hetairai*. There's no point objecting. It won't get you anywhere. You'll just have to suck it up. Medea in Euripides' play of that name sums things up as follows:

> A man, when he's tired of the company of those in his home,
> goes out and cheers himself up […] whereas we women are
> forced to direct our attentions exclusively to one person.

Your husband will also be absent for extended periods of time whenever he's called upon to perform military service. In theory that could be at any time and at a moment's notice. On such occasions you'll enjoy some independence, although you still won't have much freedom of movement. Most of the time, you'll be reliant on your relatives (female, of course), your slaves (also female), and your children for companionship. You probably can't read, though if you're wealthy, your husband might purchase an educated slave who can read for you.

Whichever social class you belong to, you'll be expected to contribute to the welfare and prosperity of the home. One of the chief ways you can do this is by spinning and weaving. Even Aphrodite, the goddess of love and beauty, owns a distaff (hers is made out of gold), with which she spins wool or flax into yarn or thread. Odysseus' wife, Penelope, deceives her suitors by pretending to weave a shroud for her father-in-law Laertes and then undoing the weaving at night. She's told them that she will marry one of them only after she's finished weaving the shroud. She held them off for years by this ruse. Penelope might not be educated in our sense of the word, but she's obviously a lot smarter than all the suitors – 108 in total – put together.

No doubt all this sounds pretty humdrum, perhaps even stifling and stultifying, and as a twenty-first-century woman you may well find it so, but don't assume that every Greek woman will agree with you. Seclusion isn't the same as submission, and although your life revolves around the home to a degree that you may well find tedious, you need to remember that until relatively recently western women have been denied what we now consider to be basic human rights. In the UK it's only just over a century-and-a-half ago that women ceased to be under the economic and legal control of their husbands and were permitted to sue for divorce, and it's *less* than a century since women over the age of twenty-one have been entitled to vote.

Remember, too, that women are extremely vulnerable in the ancient world. Restricting them to the home and out of the public gaze is not exclusively about control. It's also about their safety and their well-being. So, although there's no question that a contemporary woman will at first find life in ancient Greece deeply frustrating, after a while she may begin to see the benefits of her seclusion.

It sounds odd to put it this way, but one of the few social outlets available to a woman is attending a funeral. That's because women handle the treatment of the dead. In particular they prepare the body for burial and accompany it to the place of interment. They also make periodic visits to the grave, depositing gifts and pouring drink-offerings known as libations.

A law court speech ascribed to a writer called Lysias describes how a married woman began a clandestine affair with her lover by exchanging glances at a funeral and, subsequently, using a slave as a go-between. The pair took what few opportunities life presented. Incidentally, the affair ended badly because the husband found them in bed together and killed the adulterer, as the law permitted.

The only other social outlet for women is provided by festivals from which men are excluded. One of the most important of these is the Thesmophoria, which is held in honour of Demeter, goddess of the harvest. As with many Greek festivals, the origin of this one is unknown, though it may have something to do with the fact that when Hades, god of the Underworld, abducted Demeter's daughter Persephone, a fissure in the earth opened up and swallowed her. That's because pigs are thrown down into a fissure at the Thesmophoria. Three days later women descend to retrieve the rotting flesh. This and other festivals give women an opportunity to get out of the house and associate with other women, and though ritual predominates, you'll find there are plenty of opportunities for the exchange of gossip.

How husbands treat their wives

You're just going to have to accept the fact that your husband will be leading a completely independent life, including having sex with any woman he chooses, so long as she isn't freeborn. As I've already indicated, Greek society operates solidly on the principle of the double standard. In particular, it's totally legit for him to sleep with a *hetaira*.

Having what we would call 'an affair' isn't an option for either a husband or a wife. In Athens, if a wife and her lover are caught *in flagrante delicto*, her husband is permitted to kill the adulterer and required to divorce his wife. If the husband doesn't immediately divorce his wife, he is liable to be stripped of his citizenship.

An adulterous man who isn't caught *in flagrante delicto* but pronounced guilty in a court of law will merely face a fine payable to the aggrieved husband, his offence being regarded as more excusable than the woman's for reasons I'll explain in a moment. A woman found guilty of adultery is debarred from all forms of public religion. Whether she's also debarred from participating in household religion is unknown. She's also prohibited from wearing jewellery, which means that everyone knows what she's done. If she violates this law and wears jewellery, anyone who wishes – that's the legal phrase – is free to tear her clothing and beat her.

Adultery is regarded as a more serious crime than rape. That's because adultery may lead to the production of an offspring whom a husband believes to be his biological heir, whereas when a rape has occurred, the husband knows that the offspring of such an act isn't his.

Prostitutes, called *pornai,* are readily available and soliciting isn't a criminal offense. In fact, brothels support the public exchequer by paying a state tax. You can even prostitute your own daughter, if you so choose, but you can't prostitute your son. If you do, the law will punish you severely. In addition, your son won't be required to support you in your old age, as is his obligation otherwise.

Human nature being what it is, there must be some wives who give their husbands a hard time for their infidelity, even though it isn't possible for a wife to sue for divorce on grounds of mental or physical cruelty. When the wife of a politician and general called Alcibiades tried to leave him, he dragged her back home by her hair, thereby publicly shaming her. I often wonder whether Penelope gave Odysseus a piece of her mind when he got home in reprisal for his dalliances. I certainly hope so.

Your husband is probably at least ten years older than you are. Though we don't know the precise age-band covered by marriageability, it seems to have extended from seventeen to thirty-five in the case of a man and from thirteen to twenty-five in the case of a woman. Whereas a male is free to contract a marriage from eighteen onwards, a female of any age can do so only at the instigation of her father or legal guardian.

The Greeks see nothing objectionable in what we would regard as a deeply asymmetrical relationship. On the contrary, they approve of it. Given the age difference between husband and wife, you must expect a degree of paternalism in your husband's treatment of you. An imaginary character called Ischomachus in a treatise by a pamphleteer called Xenophon says he wasn't able to have a rational conversation with his wife until he had 'tamed' her, by which, I suspect, he means discipline her to his view of how she should behave. Once he had completed this task, Ischomachus was able to explain to his wife her duties as mistress of the house. The crusty old sod urged her not to apply makeup but instead to acquire a healthy complexion by kneading dough and folding up linen.

Domestic abuse must occur, though how frequently and with what severity we don't know. When Lysistrata, in Aristophanes' play of that name, criticises the way men are running the war, her husband bawls, 'Get back to your weaving, woman, or I'll give you a black eye!'

If you happen to live in Sparta, you'll probably be a bit older when you marry and therefore be closer in years to your husband. As a result he'll treat you more as his equal. It's not surprising, therefore, that Spartan women have a reputation for being strong-willed, independent and outspoken. They are the only Greek women we know of who are permitted to own property in their own name. We'll meet a Spartan woman later.

The irony is that if your husband is poor, you'll probably enjoy more freedom than if he's wealthy. That's because you may have to go out either to work or to perform routine outdoor tasks, such as fetching water from the communal fountain or well. 'Who can prevent the wives of the poor going out whenever they want?' Aristotle asked, evidently with a touch of exasperation. At least if you do have to carry home buckets of water from the local fountain every day, you'll have the opportunity to mingle with women of your own social rank.

Although Greek society is set up in such a way that women are either marginalised or excluded from public life, we shouldn't assume that they are all docile and uneducated. To quote Medea one more time, 'Here and there you might find one or two women who aren't complete ignoramuses.'

If the impressive list of forthright and outspoken women in drama is anything to go by – think of Antigone, Clytemnestra, Hecuba, Lysistrata, Medea and Phaedra – at least some Greek women know how to give as good as they get. Such characters may be exceptional but they are surely drawn from real life.

Does all this mean that there's no such thing as true love between a husband and wife and that conjugal bliss is unattainable? It's impossible to answer that question because we don't have any testimony from either a husband or a wife that describes their relationship. Romance doesn't feature in the literature of this period and we don't have any love letters either. All we have are generalised accounts written by men in fictionalised or philosophical contexts. A treatise written by Plutarch, a moralist and biographer, speaks eloquently of the importance of 'like-mindedness' between spouses, and it's tempting to infer that his view would have been shared by many couples in antiquity. But certainty lies beyond our grasp.

How women give birth

Most women give birth in the home by sitting on a birthing stool. The stool has a circle cut out of the central portion so that the newborn baby can emerge by the force of gravity and be caught by the midwife. A few women give birth outdoors, leaning against a tree. That's how Leto, the mother of the twins Artemis and Apollo, gave birth on the island of Delos.

Giving birth is a moment of intense apprehension for all the household, primarily because of the high incidence of deaths of women in labour; perhaps as high as ten to twenty per cent. The risk to the newborn is even greater. This is partly because there's so little understanding of the need for hygiene and practically no means of providing it anyway. The dangers of childbirth are reflected in the belief that it releases *miasma* or pollution into the household. This means that before, during, and after birth rituals must be performed to prevent this highly contagious element from seeping into the community.

Only women are permitted to attend a delivery, except on rare occasions when a male obstetrician is at hand, though only a minority of households have sufficient resources to engage the services of such a person. For the most part, the burden of securing a viable delivery and safeguarding the life of the mother will fall on the shoulders of a midwife, who will be introduced to the pregnant woman some time before her delivery so that a relationship of trust can build up. This means that midwives occupy a very important place in the community.

It partly falls upon the midwife to determine whether the newborn baby should be raised or 'exposed': that is to say, removed from the household and abandoned, perhaps in some well-frequented area where a childless individual may happen upon it and rescue it. We don't have any idea what percentage of newborns are exposed. In Greek drama and novels it's a relatively common practice, but this may be misleading.

Sickly babies and girls are most at risk of being exposed: girls because they contribute less than boys in economic terms and because they need to be provided with a dowry. If a girl doesn't receive a dowry, she may remain unmarried and be a burden to her family all her life. A litigant in a speech by the orator and politician Demosthenes says, 'Who would ever receive a woman without a dowry from a penniless father?' It's a sad fact of life that many households probably don't have the resources to raise more than a single daughter.

There's one mitigating factor in all this. Abhorrent though exposure is to our modern sensibility, many babies will be rescued by childless couples due to the high level of sterility and infertility.

Because of the high incidence of neonatal mortality, the Greeks don't immediately incorporate newborn babies into their household. On the fifth day after birth, they perform a curious ritual known as the *Amphidromia*, which means 'Running around'. It is so named because either the father or the mother runs around the hearth holding the baby. The purpose is to purify the baby by bringing it into contact with fire and placing it under the protection of Hestia, goddess of the hearth. The baby is now a fully-fledged and legitimate member of the household. At the *Amphidromia*, or at a subsequent ritual performed on the tenth day after birth, it will be given its name.

Newborn babies are wrapped in swaddling bands from head to toe in the belief that this will prevent them from distorting their limbs by vigorous movement. Swaddling has a very long history and medical opinion to this day remains divided as to its efficacy.

How you treat your children

Childhood is a lot shorter in ancient Greece than it is in our society. In fact, there are some grounds for suggesting that childhood, as we think of it today, namely as a discrete period of life stretching well over a decade, is a relatively modern cultural phenomenon. The second thing is that ancient Greece isn't a child-oriented culture. You certainly aren't going to be mollycoddling your children and there's no equivalent of the soccer mum. I suspect that few parents make the emotional well-being of their offspring a particularly high priority. That doesn't mean they don't care for them. It simply means that emotional well-being isn't on their radar.

Children play mainly with their siblings. Playdates are a rarity, except when cousins and other relatives visit. Sleepovers are also rare. There are no such things as playgrounds, though children frequently play on swings and seesaws on their parents' property.

Well-to-do parents assign the care of their children to nurses, usually servile. A nurse may form as close an attachment to the child under her care as does the mother. The fact that Odysseus' nurse, Eurycleia, recognises the scar on his thigh – an intimate part of his anatomy – when she washes him, even though he is disguised as a beggar, is a strong indication of that.

If you're poor, you'll put your children to work as soon as they can stand on two legs. Whatever education they receive will be subsidiary to their need to become productive as early as possible.

In case you haven't guessed it yet, there's absolutely no place for sentimentality in ancient Greece. Don't hesitate to give your child a good thrashing even for a minor disobedience. He or she is very much an adult in-waiting and the sooner childhood is disposed of the better it is for everyone. Besides, life is short and there's little point in wasting it growing up when you could be doing something far more interesting.

Judging from objects placed in children's graves, the most popular toys are rattles and terracotta dolls with moveable arms tied with string. The latter are so plentiful that they may well be mass-produced. Older children play with knucklebones and dice. Extracurricular activities for girls include singing in a choir and for boys athletic training.

There's no knowing what it's actually like being a child in ancient Greece. We don't have a single statement from a child, other than the artificial words that are put into their mouths by the dramatists. Some philosophers discuss how to raise children but no doubt they are all oldish men, who may or may not be parents themselves. Childhood may sound a bit dreary compared with what it's like today, but who's to say that the absence of stimuli like cellphones, computers, iPads and video games doesn't make children a lot more self-reliant and contented?

One last point. As is true in many societies, stepmothers get a very bad rap. When a young wife called Alcestis is about to die in Euripides' *Alcestis*, she says to her husband Admetus, 'I beg you not to marry again. A stepmother who is ill-disposed towards her stepchildren is as vicious as a viper.' A particularly nasty example is Phaedra, who falls in love with her stepson, Hippolytus. In Euripides' *Hippolytus* she hangs herself after being rejected, leaving behind a suicide note in which she accuses him of rape.

How you educate your children

Both boys and girls spend their early years with their mothers and, if they have one, with their nurses, in a separate part of the house known as the *gynaikônitis*, or women's quarters. Except in Sparta, where boys are in essence the property of the state from the age of five onwards, there's no public education system in ancient Greece, which means there's no legal requirement to send your child to school. As a result, parents are entirely responsible for the upbringing of their offspring. Since fathers are largely absent, sometimes for long periods of time, mothers have to do much of the supervision.

You won't be expected to give much thought to your daughter's education. It's sufficient if she learns how to spin, weave, cook, keep the domestic slaves in line, and generally be capable of running the household. A boy's formal education begins around the age of seven and generally ends around the age of fourteen. We have no idea what percentage of the population was educated in the formal sense of the word.

Though privately run, Athenian schools are subject to a strict code of practice. They are not permitted to open before dawn and they must close before sunset. This is to ensure the boy's safety, not least to avoid exposing him to pederasts.

If you're wealthy, your son will probably receive individual instruction from a slave. If you're poor, he will be barely educated, merely learning a craft or trade. As the comic dramatist Aristophanes makes clear in *Knights*, however, even a humble sausage seller, one of the lowest of the low, is expected to know how to read and write, though it's unclear how someone from an impoverished family would become literate. The fact remains, though, that a majority of the Athenian *Dêmos* needs to be literate at least at the basic level in order to participate in the running of the state and the empire. Boys learn to write on wax tablets, since these can be wiped and reused multiple times. Papyrus, the chief writing material, from which our word 'paper' comes, is a luxury item since it has to be imported.

Seated man
reading a scroll.

Education consists primarily of reading, writing and drawing. Well-to-do boys learn how to play a musical instrument, especially the lyre and the double-reeded pipes. Mathematics is not seen as an essential part of the curriculum.

Committing poetry to heart is an important attainment. We hear of fathers who require their sons to learn the whole of Homer's *Iliad* and *Odyssey*; some 25,000 lines in total. The Greeks revere Homer as a storehouse of wisdom on practically every subject under the sun. This is due to the fact that 'in his genius he wrote about nearly all the things that concern human beings,' as Xenophon tells us.

Knowledge of Greek poetry is essential if you want to join in the games that are played at a symposium, i.e. drinking party, with cultivated drinkers, as I'm sure you will. One game requires a player to quote a line from a poem and the next player to quote a line which begins with the letter that ended the line just quoted, and so on and so forth till only one player is left in the game. Poetry can even be a life-saver. Many of the Athenians who will be captured by the Syracusans after the failure of their expedition to Sicily will owe their release to the fact that they are able to recite the choral odes of Euripides. The Syracusans are absolutely crazy about Euripides. Imagine getting out of jail by being able to recite a sonnet of Shakespeare in our society.

Bust of Homer.

38

Girls receive only a basic education, mainly in household management. A few aristocratic girls officiate on behalf of female deities especially at festival time.

Both boys and girls undergo indoctrination into what we might broadly call the ideology of the Athenian *polis*. This is so that they will grow up to accept their identity as members of a unique community with its characteristic set of rules and laws, its distinctive history, and its specific set of values. This includes awareness of Athens' proud tradition of giving aid to suppliants. Athenian youths, known as ephebes, undergo indoctrination through a programme known as the *ephêbeia*, which marks the transition from adolescence to adulthood. An ephebe, in other words, is someone on the cusp of adulthood. The *ephêbeia* consists mainly of military training, plus instruction in Athens' military history.

What we would call tertiary education, viz. the equivalent of university, is expensive and available only to the élite. Some wealthy young men study with teachers known as sophists. 'Sophist' means literally 'a person who practises wisdom'. In reality, however, sophists specialise in the teaching of rhetoric. It's their function to coach young men in the art of persuasion, an invaluable asset in both the political and legal arena.

A lot of people look down their noses at sophists. They think they're a thoroughly bad influence. They claim they teach their students how to make the weaker argument appear the more convincing, irrespective of its merits, and indeed there's some truth in that. The most vocal opponent of sophistic training is Socrates, who objects to the fact that they charge for their services and are indifferent to the truth. His prejudice has coloured our appreciation of their contribution to education for all time. Likewise Xenophon, who followed in Socrates' footsteps, claimed that sophists were only interested in profit and that there wasn't a single wise man among them. Hence, the opprobrium that attaches to our use of the word 'sophistic', meaning an argument that is clever-clever but lacks merit. That's most unfortunate, because some sophists were highly original thinkers.

Moving on to the personal side of life, there is no dating scene in ancient Greece. Well-to-do girls are closely supervised because of the high importance attached to their virginity. If the groom discovers that his bride isn't a virgin on their wedding night, he has the right to declare the marriage null and void. The girl will then be blacklisted and her family humiliated.

Raising Spartan children

You know the old saying, 'Don't mess with a Spartan mother'? Well, it's true. They're the ones who made Sparta the city it is today. It would be nothing without them. Spartan girls are taught from childhood to be servants of the state. That's why they train and do strenuous gymnastic exercises, because they're the ones upon whom the future of the state most depends. No other Greeks give any thought to their daughters' education. I'm not talking about learning how to read and write. I'm talking about what they consider to be a *real* education: learning stories about Sparta's history, its gods, its traditions, its values, its ideology, and so on, and generally toughening up. Spartans are the proudest people on the face of the earth. And it's all due to their mothers.

Spartan girls exercise regularly so that they'll be in tiptop condition when they get pregnant. They need to be fit so that they will give birth to strong and healthy babies who will grow up to be fearless warriors. Spartan mothers are highly respected for this reason. If a Spartan woman dies giving birth to a boy, she's permitted to have a tombstone with her name inscribed upon it. That puts her on a level with soldiers who die fighting for their country. No one else in Sparta is accorded such an honour.

Every newborn Spartan baby has to be inspected by the Elders of the Tribes to determine whether it is worth rearing. The inspection takes place immediately after birth. If it isn't perfect, it will be abandoned in the foothills of Mount Taygetus at a place called the Kaiades. The elements and the wild animals will end its life. In reality, it's a merciful death because a Spartan child who isn't perfect is regarded as useless both to itself and to the state.

Both the *oikos* and the state share in the task of child-rearing, though mainly it's the job of the state. The state comes first and the household a distant second. When a boy turns five, the state takes over his education and he's placed in the care of an older lad. His job is to mould the boy into a hardened brute, who will be able to withstand any amount of pain and inflict it on others when ordered to do so.

Spartan youths become full citizens around the age of twenty when they graduate from the *krupteia*, meaning 'the secret thing', i.e. the secret police, of which more later. They become known as 'equals' or *homoioi*, because they all have equal rights of citizenship. They join a dining club and from then onwards their first commitment is to their messmates, as they'll fight alongside them all their lives. This is signalled by the fact that on their wedding night Spartan bridegrooms spend only a short amount of time with their brides before returning to the company of their messmates.

It goes without saying that Spartan mothers are immensely proud of their offspring. There's a story of one mother whose son was competing in the footrace at the Olympic Games and who disguised herself as a man so she could see him compete. However, she was exposed – literally – when she jumped up and down with joy to celebrate his victory. She was the first and the last woman to witness an event at the Olympic Games.

Spartan hoplites carry a bronze shield with the letter lambda for 'Laconia' [the territory occupied by the Spartans] inscribed on it. Their cloak is dark red so that it won't show any blood if their owner is wounded. It's a great honour for a Spartan to die in battle, whereas if he flees and throws away his shield, he will never live down the disgrace. 'With your shield or on it,' was the stern injunction of one Spartan mother to her son, meaning either return with your shield or be carried back home dead on top of it.

Spartan wives don't see much of their husbands. Spartiates – that's another name for the Equals – owe their primary obligation to the state. There's an old joke that the only time a Spartiate truly relaxes is when he goes off to war. It indicates the respect that other Greeks have for Spartan soldiers.

As I've mentioned, Spartan wives are closer in age to their husbands and can own property in their own name. It's doubtful whether there are women anywhere in the Greek world who enjoy as much freedom. They aren't backward in coming forward either. There's a story about a wife who was asked if her husband had made love to her the previous night. 'It wasn't that way around. I made love to him,' she promptly replied.

It's true that Sparta can be a bit dull at times – it doesn't have all the distractions and entertainments and luxuries that Athens has – but it has plenty of festivals, even if they aren't quite as spectacular. From a Spartan perspective, the Athenians do everything to excess.

Women's Lib doesn't exist but a few years after you arrive a Spartan princess called Cynisca – her name means 'female puppy' – will make it her life's ambition to win first prize at the Olympic Games by 'competing' in the four-horse chariot race. That's the only way a woman can win at the Games, because the prize in this event is awarded to the owner of the team of horses, not to the charioteer. Cynisca won't be able to watch the race if she does compete – remember that women can't attend the games – but she'll become famous all the same. Some people say that Sparta is changing, but don't hold your breath.

What to do if you don't have any children

One option for a childless man is to impregnate a slave. The downside with this, however, is that his offspring won't be entitled to claim Athenian citizenship. He or she will be regarded as illegitimate. A better option is to adopt, preferably a male of adult years. This will be a *quid pro quo* arrangement. The adoptive father will expect his adopted son to look after him and his wife in old age, see that they're both honourably buried, and visit their graves on a regular basis so that they flourish in the Underworld. In other words, the adopted son will perform all the duties and responsibilities that a biological son performs on behalf of his parents. That's why it's better if he is already an adult. If you adopt a child when you're already advanced in years, he might not be old enough to perform his duties when you kick the bucket.

Your adopted son will become your sole heir and beneficiary. The law requires an Athenian father to leave his entire fortune to his son or sons, irrespective of whether they are biological or adopted. This means that he won't have any anxiety that you might renege on the deal and leave your estate to the cats' home, say.

I'm not suggesting that adoptive parents and adopted sons don't feel deep affection for one another. One reason why a strong bond is likely to develop is because an adopted son has to renounce all legal ties to his biological family and isn't permitted to inherit from his biological father.

Adoption in ancient Greece is a decidedly good institution. On the one hand, it acts as a kind of insurance policy for those who have no one to look after them in old age, and, on the other, it provides young men who would otherwise be poor with greater financial security. That's because a young man is unlikely to put himself up for adoption unless he is assured of improving his financial lot in life by exchanging fathers, so to speak. It would be logical to assume that many adoptions take place between relatives, though we don't know whether this is actually the case.

There are no adoption agencies, so if you actually want to adopt a baby, the best thing to do is to visit a well-frequented spot where unwanted babies are abandoned. You might even try the local refuse dump. Many adopted children are given names with the prefix *kopros*, which means 'dung, refuse,' indicating where they were found. Apparently no opprobrium attached to such castaways. There's even an Attic *deme* called 'Dung'.

It's pretty clear that the Greeks favour a son over a daughter. I don't want to suggest that this was universally the case, but it may well have been the majority preference. Tellingly, the historian Herodotus writes of a man 'who died childless, leaving behind only a daughter.'

But what if you have no male heir and only a daughter or, worse, several daughters? In that case your estate will become 'attached', as the saying goes, to your eldest daughter, who will be strongly expected, if not required, to marry a close relative. This is so that your *oikos* will survive.

Only a childless man is permitted to leave his estate to whomever he wishes. Aristotle, who had no heir, left the bulk of his considerable fortune to his mistress, though he asked to be buried beside his wife. What a solid gent!

How a woman can beautify herself

Greek men find pale women very attractive, so I suggest you apply white paste to your face and arms. If you acquire a cosmetic mortar and pestle, you'll be able to mix the paste yourself. I also urge you to stay out of the sun as much as possible. The last thing you want is a tan!

Greek women wear their hair long. Sometimes they apply henna to colour it. Most of the time they wear it piled on top of the head, often in braids, which they keep in place with bronze or bone hairpins. If your hair is thin, you can buy a hairpiece. Some are quite fancy.

Combs are made out of wood or ivory. Mirrors are made out of bronze. Bronze isn't half as reflective as glass, of course, but if you keep it shiny, it serves the purpose well enough. If you want to make a fashion statement buy a pair of platform shoes to increase your height. Greek men like tall women, not that I'm encouraging you to pander to the male gaze.

Most women own an assortment of jewellery, including rings, necklaces, bracelets and earrings. If it's costly, it will serve as part of the dowry, in which case it will remain as an heirloom in the wife's family and be handed down through the generations.

Both men and women use perfume. This isn't only for cosmetic purposes. Greeks don't bathe very often. I recommend imported perfume containing either frankincense or myrrh because it's stronger than the local stuff. You can store it in a little round bottle known as an *alabastron*.

Men are bearded and wear their hair long. Female slaves are required to crop their hair as an indication of their servile status.

Getting married

When the father or the guardian of the future bride and groom have come to an agreement regarding the size of the dowry, a betrothal ceremony takes place. The bride's father or guardian promises to hand over his daughter or charge 'for the ploughing of children.' It's a revealing turn of words, which indicates that procreation is the primary function of marriage. The bride doesn't need to be present because her consent to the union isn't required. Nor, for that matter, is she permitted to oppose it. Brides rarely get the opportunity to exercise any choice in the selection of their husbands.

As I've indicated, there's an almost complete lack of evidence for romantic ties between men and women, though we should be wary of assuming that none exists. In Sophocles' *Antigone*, Haemon, who is engaged to Antigone, kills himself after his father has condemned his bride to death. But the pair never declare their undying love for one another. In fact they never address each other during the play, which means that the depth of their attachment remains a mystery. So we don't know whether Haemon commits suicide because he can't go on living without Antigone or simply because he wants to punish his father. It isn't until the rise of the Greek novel, four hundred years later, that romantic love begins to feature. The most popular example of the genre is Longus' *Daphnis and Chloe*, which I highly recommend.

On the day of the wedding, the bride and groom take a bath – separately and in their own homes – in water drawn from a sacred spring, its purpose being ritual purification. Subsequently a wedding feast takes place in the bride's house. The bride sits veiled in the company of her female relatives, including the equivalent of her maid of honour. At nightfall, the groom conveys her in a horse-drawn cart to his home. The pair are accompanied by a torchlight procession, during which wedding hymns are sung in honour of Hymen, the god of marriage.

Upon entering the groom's house, the bride is conducted to the hearth, where she is placed under the protection of Hestia and other household deities, just like a newborn babe. This signals that she has

Bride and groom.

been formally incorporated into her new home. Bride and groom are showered with nuts and dates, the ancient equivalent of confetti and symbolic of fertility and wealth.

No priest or priestess is present, nor is any state official in attendance. There is nothing comparable to a religious service. To our best knowledge, there is no exchange of vows or anything equivalent to a marriage register. The climax to the proceedings comes when the bride removes her veil and reveals her face to the groom.

The final act takes place when the newlyweds enter the bedroom. As the door closes, relatives and well-wishers sing a hymn known as the *epithalamion*, which means literally 'at the bridal chamber'. The next day the wedding guests return to the house with gifts. `

The newlyweds are unlikely to enjoy much privacy. The bride may find herself living with the groom's parents and his siblings, a sister-in-law, an ageing aunt or two, and one or more grandparents. Privacy in general is in short supply in Classical Greece.

The Wedding Day

Imagine now the plight of a young Athenian girl aged thirteen or fourteen, who is about to be married. She's excited, but she's anxious as well. She's only met her husband-to-be twice since getting betrothed and never in private, so she's not had a one-on-one conversation with him and knows little about him, other than what her father or guardian has told her. He's likely to be almost twice her age.

When she pictures what's going to happen tomorrow, she keeps thinking of the story of Persephone and Pluto. Persephone, daughter of Demeter, goddess of the corn, was walking in the fields, innocently plucking flowers, not a care in the world, when – voilà! – a dirty great hole appeared at her feet and out popped Pluto, who forcibly grabbed hold of her and whisked her down to the Underworld to make her his bride without so much as a by-your-leave. On her arrival in his mouldy kingdom, Pluto added insult to injury by tricking her into eating five pomegranate seeds. Once you've had a meal down in Hades, or even just a snack, you become the property of Hades, and in her case of Pluto. A few Athenian girls might think that marrying the king of the Underworld is a dream come true, but the majority would regard it as an absolute nightmare.

As at a modern Greek wedding so at an ancient one; there's a lot of tasty food to eat and quality wine to drink and everybody will be very merry. It's the moment when she finds herself alone with her groom that makes a bride fearful, since she's never had any experience of sex; not so much as an amorous peck on the cheek.

I imagine her nurse has said to her, 'Whatever you do, don't shrink away when Speusippus puts his arms around you. That'll make him angry. You don't want to start your marriage on the wrong foot. And don't ever turn your back on him either. Whenever he wants it, you just let him have it.' But what does the average nurse know about the situation a young bride is facing?

It all happens so quickly. One moment the barely adolescent girl is playing with her baby sister, tying ribbons in her hair. The next her father turns up, to inform her that she's going to be married to a perfect stranger in Gamelion, the month when most weddings take place.

On the day of the wedding the bride will leave her parents' house and go to live with a man whom she barely knows. Rather like in the story of Persephone and Pluto, her husband will take her to some dark place and then in an instant the world of her childhood will shatter. In fact her childhood has already ended: it did the moment her father or guardian broke the news of her engagement to her. The story of Persephone and Pluto is on one level about the sudden death of a girl's childhood.

Before the wedding takes place, her nurse keeps telling her that she's a silly little thing and that being anxious on her wedding night is a small price to pay for a husband, and that, if she's lucky, she'll bear lots of children. She tells her charge she'll be held in high esteem, whereas if she doesn't get married her life will be miserable and other women will look down on her. She should be grateful that her father has spent a lot of time searching for a good husband, because there's hardly any fate worse than remaining a spinster all one's life. If you do, everyone will treat you like dirt.

But that doesn't alter the fact that the girl is really scared. What if her husband doesn't like her? What if she can't stand being touched by him? What if he's abusive?

In the story, Demeter is so upset when her daughter is abducted that she grieves and neglects to look after the crops. As a result, a famine occurs and both humans and animals starve. Eventually Zeus intervenes. He strikes a deal with Pluto: Persephone will stay with her husband for five months of every year and return to Olympus to live with her mother for the other seven. That's how the seasons arose. The five months when Demeter is grieving correspond to the winter and the seven months when she rejoices correspond to the summer. But the myth not only explains the change in the seasons, but also highlights the poignancy that a mother experiences when she is separated from her daughter.

How to treat your domestic slaves

Though the law permits you to abuse your slaves both physically and sexually, it would be only natural if you develop a relationship with a person with whom you spend long hours every day. And it's obvious that your domestic slaves will work better if you act humanely towards them. A child and its nurse, and a boy and his *paidagôgos*, the slave who accompanies him outside the house and attends to his welfare, are likely to enjoy a close bond. So, too, is a hoplite and the slave who accompanies him on a military campaign. Hardly surprisingly, in light of all this, the faithful domestic is a stock figure in the plays of Euripides.

I'm not suggesting that domestic slavery is a benign institution – abuse is commonplace – but it may be better to be a slave in Classical Athens than it will be in the Antebellum American South. One of the reasons for this is that Athenian slavery isn't racially based. Much, of course, will depend on the luck of the draw. Odysseus was a good master to those of his slaves who remained faithful to him during his twenty years' absence, but how typical is he? We might note, too, that he hanged all the female slaves who slept with the suitors.

There are so many questions we can't answer. What happens to elderly slaves who have outlived their years of usefulness? In theory they can be abandoned or denied food and shelter at the discretion of their owners. Some, however, are treated with affection to the end. This is indicated by grave markers that have come to light in family plots inscribed with servile names.

There's no getting away from the fact that slavery will require you to make a huge adjustment and that you will encounter and witness many instances of cruelty. There may even be moments when you are tempted to abuse a slave yourself. I know this may sound shocking, but over time you may well acquire a different mindset in keeping with the spirit of the times.

Pets

Lots of Greeks own pets. You may recall the story of Odysseus' dog, Argos, which recognises its master after a twenty-year separation and then instantly expires, presumably due to a heart attack caused by its excitement at its master's return. It's one of the most poignant moments in the *Odyssey* and it suggests that man's best friend is already man's best friend back in the eighth century BCE.

Dogs are expected to protect your house, as they are today, and they are taken out hunting. Young children like to play with ducks and geese. The myth of Zeus seducing Leda in the guise of a swan might suggest that some girls form intimate attachments to their pets.

If you're crazy rich, you might own a string of racehorses, which you enter in the Olympic Games or in some other equestrian competition held at any of the other major sporting venues.

Pets in general, however, don't receive anything like as much care and attention as they do in our society. Many of them are mistreated and most of them are malnourished. It goes without saying that there aren't any vets, except perhaps for those expensive racehorses.

What it's like being elderly

Being elderly is a mixed bag at best. You'll feel a lot of aches and pains, but let's not forget that you've been dealing with a lot of aches and pains all your life. The only difference is that as you age it will get a lot worse. Both your sight and your hearing will be impaired. Almost inevitably you'll be leaning on a stick or hobbling on a crutch. You'll probably begin demonstrating the symptoms of old age by the time you're in your forties or even earlier, assuming you survive that long. Life will become a whole lot tougher, as I keep warning you. The medical profession doesn't concern itself with the elderly and there is no such science as geriatrics or gerontology. If your household is strapped for cash or short of resources, you're at the bottom of the food chain, both literally and metaphorically.

That said, as a senior citizen you'll be looked up to and treated with respect. That would be especially true if you lived in Sparta. The Spartans are famous for deferring to their elders. They stand aside for them in the street. Imagine that! Well, according to a pamphleteer called Isocrates, Athenians in the old days were just as respectful of their elders, but today it's a different story. The comic poet Aristophanes tells an anecdote about a toothless old man who was dazzled by the rhetorical fireworks of his young legal adversary and cheated of the money he had set aside to pay for his own coffin. The anecdote may well be true. In that respect the Athenians aren't so different from us.

You'll certainly be put to full use as a grandparent. Though there's no old-age pension, you can support yourself by jury service, which pays a drachma a day, though the work isn't guaranteed. And it's only an option if you live in Athens or close by. If you live in the countryside, you'll hardly want to trek to Athens in the hope that you'll be called to serve. Maybe you'll be able to continue working on the land, like Laertes, Odysseus' elderly father, who tends vines on what is evidently now his son's estate. In Odysseus' absence Laertes seems to have handed over control of the household to his grandson Telemachus. In other words, he has retired. The word 'retirement' has no equivalent in Greek, for the obvious reason that it is extremely rare.

Homer describes a happy old age as 'glistening' or 'shiny'. Quite what he means by that is unclear, but it does at least suggest that longevity isn't without its compensations, so long as you are well-heeled.

Shopping

Where to shop

If you live in Athens, you'll probably shop in the Agora, unless you have a decent-sized plot where you can grow all your vegetables and other foodstuffs. Even so, I'm sure you'll want to try something exotic from time to time. Pericles claimed that all the products of the world are on sale in Athens, and although that's a slight exaggeration, his claim is well-founded.

Since well-to-do women are expected to remain inside the home, the majority of shoppers are men. They are often accompanied by their slaves, whom they treat as shopping carts. Trusted slaves, however, are sent out to shop by themselves.

Traders set up stalls or tents in the Agora. Such structures don't leave any traces in the archaeological record, but we read of designated areas called 'circles', where traders who sell the same product gather. Purveyors of fish, meat, wine, cheese, slaves, and so forth all have their own circles. So, too, do cobblers, tailors, perfumers, barbers, and jewellers. Then as today, barber shops are great places to learn the latest gossip. You'll recall that it will be in a barber shop that news of the Sicilian disaster will first reach Athens.

There are also neighbourhoods outside the Agora where particular trades flourish. Metalworkers are to be found on a hill on the west side of the Agora, appropriately close to the temple of Hephaestus, the patron god of metalworking. Sculptors have their premises on the slopes of the Areopagus, the hill to the northwest of the Acropolis. Vendors of painted pottery, lamps, and terracotta figurines, whose manufacture requires an abundance of water, set up shop on the banks of the Eridanus River, which flows through the Ceramicus. The Ceramicus became Athens' premier burial ground precisely because of the abundance of painted pottery available there, which, as we've seen, is the most popular grave gift.

Types of vases.

We know most about the Agora in Athens because it is by far the biggest trading centre in the Classical Greek world. It's the primary market for all the members of Athens' maritime alliance, who sail there both to buy and to sell. But each of Athens' 150-odd *demes* or townships possesses its own agora, where buying and selling takes place on a much smaller scale. Agoras in the remoter areas only host markets once every few days. They resemble farmers' markets, which exist to this day both in Europe and the US. And what is true of Athens is true throughout the Greek-speaking world. Every *polis* has its own agora, which functions as the centre of commercial, as well as political and legal, activity.

Even highly skilled craftsmen are generally held in low esteem by the land-owning gentry. Among the most despised are the tanners, who reek of the animal skins which they fashion, as well as of the dung they use to soften the skins. Warning: this is an extremely class-conscious society and class-prejudice runs high.

The life of a retailer

Retailing is tough at the best of times and most retailers live from hand to mouth. The poor have to transport their wares in handcarts, setting up their stall around dawn and returning home around sunset. It's a gruelling life because they're exposed to intense heat, rain, squalls and snow. Many small enterprises are family businesses, with the elderly and small children, as well as women, pitching in. Though most retailers are men, many women, widows especially, sell goods to earn a pittance.

Trading in the Agora is strictly regulated. Market clerks ensure fair trading by using standard measurements, and any buyer who suspects fraud is free to lodge a complaint. If the retailer is found guilty of malpractice, he or she will be fined or, in extreme cases, banned from further trading.

Classical Athens has a largely monetary economy. The principal silver coin is called an 'owl'. That's because the reverse is decorated with the image of an owl, the bird that is sacred to Athena and noted for

Reverse of Athenian coin depicting an owl and sprig of olive, both symbolic of Athena.

Obverse of Athenian
coin depicting the
head of Athena.

its wisdom. The obverse depicts the helmeted head of Athena. Athens'
allies are required to trade with 'owls', so the currency circulates widely
throughout the Aegean. In rural parts of Attica and elsewhere in the Greek
world, coins are something of a rarity and barter is still commonplace.
The basic unit is the drachma, which modern Greeks were still using
until they replaced it with the euro in 2002. 'Drachma' derives from the
word *drassomai*, which means 'I grasp'. That's because, before coinage
was invented, the currency was a grasp, or handful, of six spits, known
as *oboloi*.

Food and Diet

What you'll eat

The Greeks eat only two meals a day: a fairly light meal early on called *ariston*, which consists of olives, cheese, honey, bread and fruit, washed down with diluted wine; and *deipnon*, a heavier meal in the early evening, also washed down with diluted wine. Wine, you should know, is a lot more trustworthy than water. There are no fast food outlets or restaurants, but if you get a bit peckish mid-morning, you can always grab the equivalent of a souvlaki, i.e. bits of vegetables and scraps of meat on a skewer. Wealthy people eat fish or meat for their *deipnon*. However, if you happen to be poor, sausages are readily available. The downside is that they tend to be stringy and the meat is pretty dodgy. Casseroles and stews mostly comprise beans and vegetables. There's no chocolate or sugar. Oranges, lemons, tomatoes, potatoes and rice haven't been discovered either. Salt is available but not pepper and there are no spices.

There are no two ways about it: it's going to be a challenge to get used to the cuisine. At the best it's going to taste rather bland. At the worst it'll turn your stomach. Most of what you're going to be eating is bread, olive oil, vegetables, honey, soup, porridge, eggs, and tripe. Tripe is a kind of soup made from the stomach of a cow or sheep. Bread is made from a mixture of barley, millet, oats and wheat. Because of the thinness of its soil, Attica produces only about one-tenth as much wheat as it does barley, so if you're poor, you'll be eating barley cakes most of the time. Peas and beans are plentiful, as are fruit and nuts. Birds, seafood and salted fish are a speciality. Varieties of seafood include octopus, squid, anchovies, oysters and eels.

The good news is that you won't have to count your daily calorific intake. You'll be able to consume as many calories as you can get hold of. You're almost certain to come up seriously short compared with what you normally eat. For that reason you won't see many obese people in ancient Greece.

If you're looking for *haute cuisine,* give Sparta a miss. The only Spartan dish we hear about is black soup. Its ingredients are enough to make you want to retch. These consist of beans, salt and vinegar, with a pig's leg thrown in for good measure. What gives it its distinctive flavour, however, is the blood in which these ingredients swill. When a man from Sybaris in southern Italy tasted black soup for the first time, he said, 'Now I know why the Spartans aren't afraid of dying.' Sybaris is well-known for its luxury and the Sybarite couldn't imagine anything worse than eating black soup every day of his life.

You've probably realised by now that the Greeks don't have much awareness of the need for hygiene. They prepare their meals in conditions that will literally turn your stomach. Vegetables aren't washed, and you may find yourself tucking into a rancid piece of meat or fish long after its sell-by date, though, looking on the bright side, you won't know what its sell-by date was.

Neither coffee nor tea is available. Nor is fruit juice, milkshake or selzer water. That's why diluted wine is the safest option. The Athenians import most of their wine. It arrives in amphoras transported on board ships that dock in the Piraeus. Try *grand cru* or its equivalent from the island of Chios; I'm sure you won't be disappointed, though I doubt you'll turn your nose up at wine from the islands of Lesbos or Thasos. If you're not exactly a wine buff, you'll probably be content with plonk from Kos, Rhodes or Knidos. Neither beer nor spirits are popular.

How to cook

A variety of utensils made out of terracotta are available, including saucepans, frying pans, grills and kettles. You'll be able to boil, roast or steam. Charcoal and dried twigs are the commonest fuels.

Bread is baked at home in a pottery oven on top of a charcoal brazier. Either you or your slave will pound the grain in a mortar. You can make a simple mortar out of a hollowed-out tree trunk. The technique is to roll a stone back and forth across the grain, letting the flour build up in the mortar. This may take several hours a day if you have a large household. The person grinding has to lean over while doing it, so the task can be backbreaking.

For a special occasion, you might want to hire a professional cook, though he will probably charge you an exorbitant fee for his services.

Clothing and Appearance

What to wear

The clothes that men and women wear are fairly similar. Trousers haven't been invented and there is a very limited choice of attire. One is the *chitôn*. This consists of two rectangles of linen attached together. The rectangles are either fastened at the shoulders and along the upper arms with pins or buttons or sewn together. A *chitôn* tends to be longer than the height of the wearer, which means that the extra material is folded over at the waist by means of a belt or a cord. Because linen is lightweight, the garment hugs the body. On a woman this can be quite revealing.

The other type of garment is the *peplos*. This tends to be favoured more by women than by men. It generally consists of a rectangular piece of wool, which is folded over. The sides of the two halves are fastened together at the shoulders like a sort of tube, which the wearer steps into. It's either tightened at the waist or left hanging loose, and worn ankle-length. The *peplos* is favoured by young girls, or rather by their parents, because the wool, being heavy, conceals the body. Wealthy girls wear brightly coloured *peploi* with an embroidered design along the edge.

In cold weather both men and women wear a loose-hanging woollen cloak known as a *himation*. Slaves wear short, skimpy attire, whether male or female. They're lucky if they're given a cloak to keep them warm in winter. Wool is in short supply.

Probably your clothes will be made in the home either by a slave or by a female family member. When you visit a Greek home, irrespective of its social status, you'll observe women spinning flax or wool into yarn or thread with a small staff known as a distaff. It's a pretty mindless activity, rather like chewing gum. After the spinning comes the weaving, which is done on a loom.

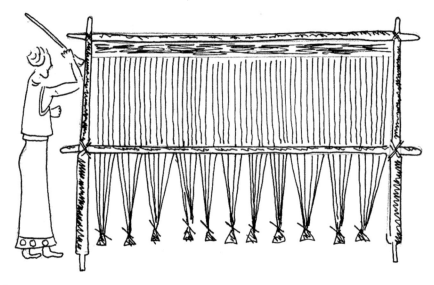

Loom.

The loom has been around for thousands of years. It consists of two upright poles supporting a crossbeam. Bundles of threads hang from the crossbeam. Each thread has a small loom weight attached to it, which holds the warp – i.e. the thread that hangs perpendicularly – under tension. This enables the weft – the thread that is stretched horizontally – to be interwoven between the warp. You'll recall that it was her skill at the loom which enabled Penelope to ward off all those suitors. She wove a design by day and unpicked it by night, pretending to be making a funeral shroud for her father-in-law.

Closets and cupboards haven't been invented so you'll have to store your clothes in a wooden chest, though I doubt you'll have an extensive wardrobe. You may possess only a single change of clothing for everyday wear, with one additional garment for special occasions, like festivals and funerals. You wash your clothes in the nearest public fountain, unless you live on the coast or in the countryside with ready access to water.

Work

What you'll think about having to work for a living

The Greeks have no word for work. *Ascholia*, which comes closest, means 'absence of leisure'. This says a lot about their priorities. Leisure from a Greek perspective is – or at least should be – the normal state of affairs, whereas work, the opposite, is abnormal. It goes without saying that they can only think in these terms because of the existence of slavery.

Athenians despise work in the sense in which we moderns use the word, and they particularly despise working for someone else. We shouldn't, however, think of them as an idle bunch. Being a citizen is a full-time job. It means attending the Assembly, serving on the Council of 500, being a magistrate, serving in the military, holding a priesthood, helping to organise a festival, performing jury service, worshipping the gods, and so on. You will also be expected to conduct yourself in your civic capacity in countless unofficial ways. For instance, you will regularly discuss the affairs of state in informal contexts such as in the Agora in the daytime or at a symposium in the evening.

Bear in mind, too, that you are not only a citizen of Athens but also a member of your *deme* or township. A *deme* functions exactly like a miniature *polis*. It has its own assembly, its own regulations, its own festivals, its own treasury, its own records, and so on, and you will be expected to take a lively interest in all this as well. So, even if you don't have to work in our sense of the word, you'll be kept busy serving your state and your *deme*. As a result, you won't be spending a lot of time at home.

Types of work

The commonest type of work is farming, much of it conducted on a very small scale. The most important agricultural products are cereals, grapes and olives. For ploughing, you'll need a team of oxen or a pair of mules. If you can't afford either, you're going to be dirt poor; in both senses. The Aegean Sea is not a rich breeding ground for fish, so fishing is on a very small scale. A large number of Greeks are involved in trade. In Athens, many traders are metics.

Craftsmen are ubiquitous, working as stonemasons, carpenters, jewellers, cobblers, blacksmiths, weavers, potters, vase painters, house painters, fullers, rope-makers, sail-makers, builders, masons, dyers, sculptors, shoemakers, sword-manufacturers; the list goes on and on. Civic building projects require a wide variety of skills.

Anyone who practises a skill, or *technê*, is a craftsman. However, it isn't only artisans who are identified as craftsmen. Those who have mastered a profession, as we would call it, including physicians and seers, are also regarded as craftsmen. Likewise, there's no hard and fast distinction between a craftsman and an artist, just as there's no hard and fast distinction between a humble artefact and a work of art in the ancient world. In that sense, it's all very democratic.

How to learn a craft

As has been true at most periods of history, craftsmen begin their apprenticeship in childhood. It's customary for a father to pass his craft on to his son. An Athenian law attributed to Solon, sometimes called the father of democracy, decrees that if a father fails to teach his son a skill, that son is not required to support him in old age. A father who is childless may either adopt a boy or else hire or purchase a slave, to whom he will then teach his craft. Herodotus informs us that in Sparta a number of skills are reserved in certain families, including those of herald, flute-player and cook, whose expertise is passed down through successive generations, and this tradition no doubt holds true generally in Greece.

Working conditions

Most craftsmen work from home in a backroom or in the courtyard. The majority of workshops are small-scale, employing perhaps two or three assistants, though a few, especially those engaged in arms manufacture, employ more than a hundred. Working conditions vary considerably from one trade to the next. Whereas being a potter or a painter of pots takes little toll on your physique, being a sculptor is extremely arduous, not least because you may also have to supervise the quarrying of the blocks yourself. Some craftsmen work in dangerous and unhealthy conditions, such as blacksmiths, who are regularly exposed to the fumes of a smelting furnace.

There are no labour-saving devices – even the wheelbarrow is unknown – and the effects of exertion often result in deformities as a result of actions and movements that are repeated again and again with mind-numbing regularity. In the absence of the seven-day week, workers are reliant on festivals to provide them with an opportunity to down tools.

The status of people who work

Aristocrats pride themselves on the fact that their wealth derives from the land and, as we've seen, they look down their noses at those whom they lump together as *banausioi*, or mechanics. Aristotle claimed that the life of the craftsman was 'ignoble and inimical to virtue' and later writers make the same point. Plutarch, who lived half a millennium later, makes the crass assumption that if you're compelled to earn your living, you don't have the leisure time to attend to the higher things of life. The divine craftsman Hephaestus is mocked for his lameness, irrespective of the fact that he produces sublime works of art. Prejudice against craftsmen is further fuelled by the fact that some of them work alongside slaves. This was the condition of those sublime sculptors who worked on the Parthenon. The status of sculptors won't improve much until the Renaissance.

But though many craftsmen face a lot of prejudice, they still take considerable pride in their accomplishments. The fact that potters and painters often sign their work tells us much about their self-esteem. However, the modern cult of the artist has no equivalent. Artists certainly aren't expected to be original. They are merely expected to equal or outdo their predecessors.

Itinerants who possess highly specialised skills are treated with respect. They include seers, physicians, architects and bards. These, in Homer's words, are in such high demand that they are 'invited from the ends of the earth' and are esteemed and rewarded accordingly.

Health and Hygiene

Diseases that are rampant

You're going to find Classical Greece a lot tougher on your body than the modern world is, due partly to illness and injury and partly to the ageing process, which is far more rapid in the ancient world. Let's talk about illness first. You name it, Classical Greece has probably got it, except perhaps for syphilis and some other sexually transmitted diseases. Viral diseases are rife, including meningitis, measles, mumps, scarlet fever and smallpox. You're unlikely to have survived to adulthood without experiencing at least one life-threatening disease. In a densely populated city such as Athens, where it's difficult to dispose of waste and to obtain uncontaminated water, diseases such as cholera and typhus are common. There are no hospitals, no means of isolating those who are suffering from communicable diseases, and little understanding of how germs spread and cause diseases. The terrible plague which affected Athens at the beginning of the Peloponnesian War was remarkable only for its virulence; it carried off perhaps one-third of the population and no doubt left an equal percentage disfigured and disabled. But it was hardly an isolated occurrence. Not infrequently some other killer disease will break out in the summer months, albeit on a much smaller scale.

Whether you should consult a physician if you fall sick

Perhaps the first thing to say is that only a small percentage of the population has enough money to consult a physician. The majority relies heavily on herbal remedies.

Sometimes consulting a physician will only make things worse. I particularly urge you to steer clear of a physician if you suffer from back pain. One supposed 'cure' is to throw the patient up in the air. Another is to suspend him or her above the ground and then violently shake them. The author of a medical treatise called *Joints* notes that such treatments often attract a large crowd and become a form of entertainment. 'It's the kind of thing that people talk about forever,' he writes, 'quite indifferent as to whether the procedure works or not.'

A popular medical procedure is bleeding, which is thought to restore the balance between the four humours that reside inside the body by removing excess blood. The theory of the four humours derives from Hippocrates, the legendary founder of modern medicine and the author of the Hippocratic Oath, still observed in a modified form to this day. Incidentally, nothing much is known about Hippocrates, other than that he lived (probably) in the first half of the fifth century on (probably) Cos, an island off the modern-day Turkish coast.

If you fall sick, you might prefer to visit one of the many sanctuaries – there are some 200 in all scattered throughout the Greek world – dedicated to Asclepius, the god of healing. Asclepius came to prominence in the middle of the fifth century. He's therefore a latecomer to the pantheon and doesn't live on Mount Olympus. The story goes that he was originally a human physician, whom Zeus struck with his thunderbolt in punishment for having resurrected someone from the dead. One of his most important sanctuaries is at Epidaurus, on the northeast coast of the Peloponnese, but you won't have to go that far because there's also one in the Piraeus. People with all manner of illnesses and injuries flock there. You'll see hundreds of sick people lying on stretchers or hobbling about on crutches. I doubt you will have witnessed human misery on such a scale before. At night the sick sleep in a dormitory within the sanctuary, hoping to be visited by the god in a dream.

If you're lucky enough to be visited by Asclepius, describe the encounter next day to a sanctuary attendant, who will help you interpret it. The god intervenes quite frequently, as you will see from the many dedications and inscriptions on display in his sanctuary. These have been put up by grateful patients who have experienced a miraculous cure.

I strongly recommend you throw all scepticism aside. When an Athenian woman called Ambrosia arrived at Epidaurus hoping to be healed, she laughed in disbelief on reading inscriptions describing what she thought were preposterous cures. To punish her for her insolence, the god appeared in a dream and promised to cure her if she dedicated a silver pig to him in acknowledgement of her piggish stupidity. Ambrosia did as he bid, and, as she records in the inscription she set up, instantly underwent a miraculous cure.

Sanctuaries of Asclepius don't deal exclusively in faith healing, however. Physicians are free to practise scientific medicine inside them. Surgeons work there as well, as we know from the discovery of troves of surgical instruments among their ruins. They perform operations on the stomach, the head, the eye, the womb, and so on. It's safe to say that there's little animosity between what we see as two adversarial approaches to healing. Instead, the two are judged to be complementary.

For minor complaints, I recommend you keep an assortment of herbs, drugs and salves at home. There's nothing equivalent to the pill, but a surefire method of contraception is to crush a few sprigs of Queen Anne's lace (known as *daucus carota* if you happen to be a botanist) and drop them into a beaker of diluted wine. On the whole, I wouldn't recommend you tie a hairy spider to your big toe to prevent conception, though lots of Athenian women I've met swear by it. Be sure to inscribe the terracotta bottles in which you store remedies with the name of the drug. And keep them on a shelf out of reach of small children!

Dealing with sickness

The most celebrated medical school is on the island of Cos. It was established by Hippocrates, whom I mentioned a moment ago. Those who practise in his name believe that health and sickness depend on a balance between the four humours – black bile, yellow bile, blood and water – and that it's the job of a physician to correct and maintain that balance. If, for instance, you've got too much black bile in your body, you'll suffer from depression and need to take an emetic. They also know how to set bones and perform surgery. They don't generally assist at a birth, but in a worst-case scenario they do know how to remove a stillborn baby from its mother's womb – a gruesome procedure.

Hippocratic physicians always emphasise the importance of gaining a patient's trust. They're opposed to drugs, preferring natural remedies. Often, as they point out, it's just a matter of letting nature take its course. They like to keep a daily account of the progress of a disease. They say that even if their patient dies, it's important to record his or her symptoms, since this may help physicians to discover a cure in the future. They acknowledge that there's still a lot they don't know about how the body is constructed.

Hippocratic physicians vehemently oppose the belief that *any* disease is caused by the gods. One of them wrote a treatise on what is still called the sacred disease; what we today call epilepsy. Greeks call it sacred because they believe that its symptoms, which are bizarre, must be prompted by the gods. The author proved beyond doubt, however, that epilepsy has a perfectly natural explanation. He did this by cutting open the skull of a ram that was suffering from epilepsy and demonstrating its physical abnormalities.

Of course, that doesn't mean that the gods don't have anything to do with cures. Physicians encourage their patients to pray to Asclepius because they understand that faith can be highly efficacious. It would greatly advance knowledge if they were permitted to dissect human bodies for purposes of research. That won't happen any time soon, however, owing to the religious taboo against tampering with corpses.

Beware you don't fall into the hands of a quack. There are plenty of them about. Hippocrates knew that medicine attracts a lot of lowlifes, bent on profit and exploitation. That's why he required his followers to take a sacred oath. The oath requires them to observe the principle of medical confidentiality, perform surgery only when it is absolutely necessary, never make a sexual advance to any patient, and never supply poison to terminate a life.

I'd like to say a few words about the terrible plague that attacked Athens just after the Peloponnesian War broke out. It started in the Piraeus and soon spread to Athens. It was so severe because half the population had moved from the countryside to the city to escape the invading Peloponnesian army. Consequently, the drinking water became quickly polluted.

Those who succumbed to the plague developed large boils, particularly under their arms and between their legs. They couldn't keep anything in their stomachs. They had a raging thirst and their bodies were hot to the touch. The only thing that would bring them any relief was bathing in cold water. Usually the disease ran its course in about ten days. A few of the lucky ones survived, but the majority died, some in frightful agony. Well, I say the ones who survived were the lucky ones, but they all bore marks of the disease for the rest of their lives. Many lost fingers and toes and their faces were horribly disfigured. Possibly as much as one-third of the population died. A number of physicians perished as a result of their devotion to their patients. The disease brought the best and the worst out of people.

People no longer cared about morality, calculating that they might as well do what they liked since they'd be dead before they knew it anyway. Another big problem was disposing of the dead. Most of the corpses were buried in large communal pits without any ceremony.

The plague returned the following year and again the year after. Each time, however, it was less virulent than before. It disappeared just as suddenly as it had arrived. But it has left a very dark scar on the collective memory of the Athenian people.

The sort of physical shape you're likely to be in

Be prepared to be suffering from an assortment of aches and pains, irrespective of your age. You may have broken a leg years ago and never had it properly set, with the result that it still gives you pain and makes you hobble. Analgesics don't exist, so you'll just have to grin and bear it. Or at least bear it. The only consolation is that everyone is in the same boat.

People age much more rapidly in the ancient world than they do today, due to a number of factors. These include undernourishment, overwork, maltreatment, war, environmental pollution, lack of hygiene, and the prevalence of life-threatening diseases. Life, in other words, tends to be nasty, brutish and short.

Children are particularly likely to be undernourished when food is in short supply – itself a common occurrence – and the effects of malnutrition will be with them for the rest of their lives. Vitamin D deficiency, which impedes bone growth and causes rickets, is especially common among girls, who, as I mentioned, tend to be fed less well than boys.

Ageing is a painful process. Most adults are battling with at least one chronic ailment or disability. You may find you have an assortment of scars and other markings on your body from injury or disease. Deafness and blindness are inevitable consequences of ageing but, surprise, surprise, there are no hearing aids or corrective lenses in Classical Greece.

By the time you're an adult, many of your teeth will be decaying, several will have dropped out, and still others will have been worn down to the stumps. Dentistry doesn't exist, though you might be able to engage the services of someone skilled in pulling teeth (skilled only in the sense that he will perform the extraction with extreme rapidity).

You'll need to keep alert constantly, as you'll find yourself in a very dangerous environment. Fire in the home is a perpetual hazard, due to open and unguarded hearths. Mudbrick, the commonest building material, easily erodes and may in consequence cause your roof to collapse. Dogs roam freely, many of them rabid. Carts frequently overturn, crushing passersby. Horses occasionally bolt in busy thoroughfares, mowing down pedestrians. Given the inadequacy in medical care, even a relatively minor mishap, such as a broken leg, a dislocated shoulder, or a fractured kneecap, may result in permanent injury. If it does, it may well signal the end of your working life. To give you some idea of the likelihood of your suffering injury, archaeologists calculate that ten per cent of Greek skeletons reveal fractures, and of that ten per cent four out of five are male. The only type of prosthesis available is a so-called peg leg, made out of wood and fitted to the remaining stump. Those most at risk from injury are slaves, soldiers and construction workers.

Sorry to saddle you with all this bad stuff, but it's best you know about it before you leave your cosy modern world. You'll need to be tough and resilient to survive in Classical Greece. It isn't a place for the querulous. But, as I hope you'll discover, there are many compensations and benefits as well.

The age structure of Greek society

The Greeks don't record age at death on their tombstones and we don't have a lot of evidence from physical anthropology, i.e. the study of bones, so we can talk about the age structure only in approximate terms. As I mentioned, earlier, you'll see proportionately many more young people and far fewer people over the age of forty than you do in our society. If you're a woman, don't expect to live much beyond your mid-thirties. If you're a man, you'll probably die in your mid-forties.

Achieving a ripe old age is a far greater accomplishment in ancient Greece than it is today. There's an essay by Lucian, a Greek satirist writing in the second century CE, called 'The Long Lived', which records the names of all those known to him who reached the age of eighty or beyond. He doesn't include a single woman in his list, though we should allow for the fact that women aren't public figures and so don't attract much notice. The disparity in life expectancy between the sexes is due to two main factors: firstly, boys are better fed; and secondly, girls typically become pregnant shortly after menarche and continue to give birth in quick succession, which has a debilitating effect on their bodies. It's revealing – and sobering – that surviving (only) till the age of eighty is regarded as the benchmark of an individual who has truly exceptional genes.

Social Structure

The divisions in Greek society

You're going to be part of a very hierarchical society. It's also one where everyone remains pretty much at the same level throughout their life. Upward and downward social mobility is relatively rare. The principal exceptions to this rule are those unlucky individuals who become enslaved as a result of being captured in war or kidnapped by pirates. The main division among the free citizenry is between the rich and the poor. In political parlance, the rich and the poor are known respectively as 'the few' and 'the many'. A middle class exists, but its size is disproportionately small compared with our society.

In Athens and elsewhere there are a number of aristocratic kin groups called *genê*, which exercise considerable political influence. This is despite the fact that Athens is a radical democracy, where every adult citizen has the right to speak in the Assembly. So, although all Athenians are in theory equal, some – the majority in fact – are more equal than others.

I've talked already about class prejudice, which results in considerable contempt on the part of aristocrats towards the poor. It is one of the paradoxes of a society which professes to be democratic that there is considerable underlying social prejudice. When non-aristocrats started to make their mark in the political arena about ten years ago, they had to bear a lot of flak because of their humble origins.

By any standards Athens is a free society, but as in any free society, there are limits. The Athenians fined a dramatist called Phrynichus for producing a play based around the destruction by the Persians of Miletus, a city on the coast of modern-day Turkey, on the grounds that it reminded them 'of their own troubles'. That's because Athens was an ally of Miletus. In a separate incident, a sophist called Protagoras was expelled from Athens and all his writings were burned because he questioned the existence of the gods. Most egregious of all, in twenty years' time an Athenian jury will condemn Socrates to death on several charges that include 'corrupting the youth', which I take to mean putting ideas in young people's heads.

Still, I suspect you'd much rather live in Athens than anywhere else in ancient Greece. You certainly wouldn't want to live in Sparta. The Spartan watchword *eunomia*, 'obedience to the law', is all well and good, but the flipside is total repression. Every form of dissent is censored in Sparta, and if you do visit, don't criticise the monarchy, or the social system, or the constitution, or any aspect of the establishment. Sparta is unique, incidentally, in having a dual monarchy; two kings from two different royal houses.

What it's like to be wealthy

Luxury is practically unknown, so it isn't the case that if you're wealthy, you'll live in anything remotely like what we would call comfort. You will, however, have a much better diet than you would if you were poor. For one thing you'll be able to eat fish or meat every day. That's a very big deal.

Wealth in the world of Classical Greece is more about extravagance and conspicuous display than about luxury. Whatever your means, you're still going to be stuck without running water, your only form of heating will be provided by an open hearth or a portable brazier, and your lighting will consist of lamps powered with animal fat or oil. One luxury will be taking a hot bath in a terracotta tub with water drawn from a well or a cistern and heated over your hearth. Another will be sleeping in a wooden bed with ropes to support the equivalent of a mattress, rather than on rush matting placed on the floor.

You'll certainly live in a bigger house than you will if you are poor, one that you probably inherited. Your wife, mother, and daughters will have separate quarters, known as the *gynaikônitis*. If you live in a two-storey house, you might use the upstairs as the women's quarters. You might also possess an *andrôn* or 'men's room', which you use when you're hosting a symposium, though this isn't as essential as a *gynaikônitis*.

There's not a lot money can buy. You'll own a set of decorated pottery, which you reserve for use at a symposium. This will include several drinking cups, a bowl for mixing wine and water, a water jug, a wine cooler, and so on. Many of these pots are decorated with scenes depicting a symposium, others with scenes inspired by mythology, and still others show scenes of daily life. If you die in Athens, you'll probably be buried with your fancy pottery, especially if you come to believe that life in the afterlife is one long piss up without the painful experience of a hangover, a view that is currently held by some hopefuls.

You'll own an impressive family plot on one of the main roads leading out of the city, ideally at a place where it will attract maximum attention from passers-by, though if you're a wealthy landowner, your family plot will be on your own property.

And, of course, one last thing you can do with your money is buy slaves and more slaves and even more slaves.

Charioteer.

Horse and rider.

One of the most expensive luxury items is a racehorse. Horses aren't much practical use in the Greek world, as I've said more than once, but they're the ultimate status symbol – the equivalent of owning a private jet in the modern world – even though you'll ride for pleasure, not to get from A to B. An Athenian general called Alcibiades will gain enormous fame by winning first, second and fourth prize in a single competition for the four-horse chariot race at the Olympic Games.

You might think of acquiring a few scrolls inscribed with the works of the dramatists, or perhaps the historians, or even the philosophers. Scrolls are expensive because they're written on papyrus, which has to be imported from Egypt. So you're unlikely to own very many. Only a handful of Athenians possess what we might call a library, and it won't be until the Romans arrive on the scene that the concept of the public library will come into being.

If you're super-rich, you'll be tapped for one of Athens' many liturgies, a word which means literally 'public services'. These include: being a trierarch, i.e. financing the expenses connected with fitting out a trireme and maintaining its seaworthiness; being a gymnasiarch, i.e. equipping and maintaining a gymnasium, especially by providing lots of olive oil for the athletes to clean themselves with after exercising; and being a *chorêgos*, i.e. covering all the expenses incurred in mounting a comic or tragic production. Performing a liturgy will give you the opportunity to compete with other super-rich Athenians, since it will be up to you to decide how much you spend discharging your service. So, in case you haven't guessed by now, one of the most important – arguably *the* most important – uses of your wealth is to be a shameless show-off.

And that's about it. You won't do anything that resembles work, though you may run a business, such as mining silver, with a workforce of perhaps a hundred slaves. But you'll place the business under the supervision of a trusted and educated slave. You don't want to dirty your own lily white hands with money. A general called Nicias, whom I mentioned earlier, owned 1,000 slaves, who laboured in the silver mines. He rented them out at an obol per slave per day. Nicias paid a talent – 6,000 drachmas, a huge sum – for the slave who ran his operation.

When your son is of an age to marry, you'll negotiate with another wealthy family to secure a bride who will come with a nice, fat dowry, though if your son predeceases her or divorces her, the dowry will be returned to her birth family.

What it's like to be poor

Not surprisingly, we hear virtually nothing about the lives of the poor. The élite, who do all the writing, don't find them interesting.

As an Athenian, however, you don't need pots of money to live fairly comfortably, both because of slavery and because of your empire. Your empire is a source of enormous enrichment to the citizenry, particularly to the poor, who benefit through state pay as rowers and jurors.

Many poor women are self-employed. The orator and politician Demosthenes, who lived in the fourth century, bemoans the plight of women who are forced to take up 'slavish and humiliating occupations', such as being wet-nurses, weavers and grape-pickers. They deserve our full sympathy and respect, owing both to the precariousness of their existence and to the courage with which they faced it.

Given the prevalence of illness and injury, given too the uncertainties of life, many Athenians, both male and female, are dependent on their relatives. It would be surprising if, at times of hardship, these dependents aren't resented by their benefactors.

What's it like to be a slave

What it's like to be a slave depends on many factors. To begin with, were you born into slavery or did you become enslaved later? If the former, you will be treated more harshly than a slave who had previously been free. In Homer's *Odyssey* the freeborn nurse, Eurycleia, and the freeborn swineherd, Eumaeus, both now servile, elicit respect and affection from their master.

Some slaves 'living outside', as it's called, working as ships' captains, bailiffs, accountants, bankers, and so forth. The Greeks regard direct contact with money as highly distasteful, so they use slaves to handle (literally) their finances. That's the reason why Aristotle considered banking to be the most hateful way of earning a living. Nurses, *paidagôgoi*, i.e. slaves who accompany boys outside the house, and other domestics are the next best off, not least because they are entrusted with the welfare of children. If you're the only slave your master or mistress owns, then you'll be cook, cleaner, nurse, minder, as well as fetcher and carrier, all rolled into one. Lower down the scale are those who work in agriculture. We don't know the size of the agricultural workforce of slaves but it's likely to be considerable. Worst off by far are those who toil in the quarries or the mines. They work very long shifts in difficult, dangerous and unhealthy conditions. Serious injuries are common and the majority literally drop dead after a few years.

There are no laws safeguarding slaves and you can mistreat them with impunity, though it's illegal to kill a slave, unless she or he has committed a serious crime. In practice, however, it's easy enough to bump off an insubordinate or fractious slave without the crime ever coming to light. The main deterrent is that it's a capital loss to kill your own slave. I suspect that corporal punishment is the norm rather than the exception. Xenophon ascribes the following observations to – of all people – Socrates: 'Don't masters chain slaves up to prevent them from running away and flog them to keep them from idleness? I use every kind of punishment to make them submit.'

Slaves are everywhere in the Greek world, though estimates of their number vary wildly. Xenophon believed that the ideal proportion is three slaves to one citizen. That's surely an exaggeration, but it's not inconceivable that slaves outnumber citizens by two to one. Xenophon thought that the state should own slaves. In fact Athens does, albeit in very small numbers. The state executioner, for instance, is a slave.

There's only one place where a world without slavery is envisaged, and that's in a fanciful comic context, where a character in a play imagines a society that is so technologically advanced that slaves are no longer needed. All you'll have to do is to say, 'Table, lay yourself', or 'Fish, turn yourself over and broil your back', and it does. Fat chance of that happening when you're in ancient Greece.

Finally, only a handful of slaves are able to earn their freedom. One who does so is Pasion, who works as a banker for his owner.

Athens' diversity

Athens and particularly its port city, the Piraeus, provide a home to thousands of resident aliens known as metics. This, of course, will be you status.

Very important: *You'll need to register as a metic with the eponymous archon, the magistrate who gives his name to the official year, within a month of your arrival. If you fail to do so, you'll either be deported or, worse, enslaved.*

The largest number of metics are domiciled in the port city, so you might feel more comfortable living in the Piraeus than you would in Athens. The most famous metic is, or rather will be, Aristotle, the tutor of Alexander the Great, born in Stagira in northern Greece. Metics come from all parts of the Greek-speaking world: Pontus (Black Sea coast), Ionia (west coast of modern-day Turkey and its offshore islands), Thrace (split today between Greece, Bulgaria and Turkey), many islands in the Aegean, Egypt, Phoenicia (split today between Lebanon and northern Israel), southern Italy and Sicily. They can't own property but they can apply to establish a cult in honour of some special deity whom they worship. They have to pay the metic tax, one drachma per month for a man, half a drachma for a woman, but are permitted to reside in Athens as long as they like. Many metics are engaged in manufacturing and commerce. Female metics often hire themselves out as *hetairai*. They are regarded as exotic by their clients and paid accordingly.

Athens couldn't function the way it does without its large metic population. The building accounts for the Erechtheum, the temple of Poseidon-Erechtheus on the Acropolis, list all the sums paid to individual craftsmen, approximately half of whom are metics. The Athenians aren't stupid. They fully realise that their prosperity depends on the energy and enterprise of their metic population, which is why they haven't tried to limit their number (or build a wall to keep them out).

Other than at a very bleak period of Athenian history, when Athens will be ruled by the so-called Thirty Tyrants, who suspend the democracy following its defeat in the Peloponnesian War, there is little evidence that metics experience any prejudice. Indeed, they enjoy special protection under the law. If a metic gets into difficulty, he or she can seek the services of a *proxenos*, an Athenian citizen who acts as their patron and protector. Each community of foreigners has its own *proxenos*. Unfortunately none has yet been assigned to twenty-first century ex-pats. You'll just have to keep your nose clean!

Marriage between metics and Athenians is discouraged. The offspring of the union between an Athenian and a metic cannot claim citizenship. However, cohabitation between Athenians and metics is commonplace. Pericles cohabited with a prominent and highly respected *hetaira* from Miletus called Aspasia. She's actually the only woman who lived in Athens in the fifth-century whose personality, to some small degree, is known to us. No Athenian woman is even a vague blur.

Athens isn't the only *polis* which hosts metics, though it does so in by far the largest numbers. Sparta discourages foreigners even to enter its territory, let alone reside there. No surprise there. The Spartans are intensely xenophobic. If you choose to visit Sparta, you'll stick out like a sore thumb. My advice is: stay in Athens.

Politics

What being an Athenian citizen means

Citizenship and the duties that go with it have no modern equivalent. To begin with, Greece isn't a nation state or even a country, so you're not actually a Greek citizen as such. You identify as an Athenian, or a Spartan, or a Corinthian, or a Macedonian, etc. In other words, your first allegiance is to your *polis*, or, in the case of a Macedonian, to your king. That said, you do acknowledge your common identity with other Greeks for certain limited purposes. A speaker in Herodotus' *Histories* defines Greekness as speaking the same language, worshipping the same gods, and having the same blood. That's as good a definition as any I could come up with.

Our word 'Greek' actually comes from the Latin word '*Graeci*', which is the designation that the Romans will later use of the people who call themselves *Hellênes*. '*Graeci*' is actually the name of an insignificant people who colonised the Italian mainland. It's not a term that the Greeks ever used of themselves and it isn't to this day.

You're a citizen of Athens by virtue of having a father and a mother who are both Athenian. If you're a boy, shortly after your birth your father will present you to a sub-division of the citizen body known as a *phratry*, or brotherhood, to which he belongs. Our word 'fraternal' comes from it. In the presence of his *phratry* at a festival held in honour of Apollo known as the *Apatouria,* he will declare under oath that you are the legitimate offspring of an Athenian father and an Athenian mother. He will again present you when you turn eighteen, and on this occasion the members of his *phratry* will take a vote on your legitimacy. If you pass the test, you will be enrolled as a citizen in a register kept by your *deme*. Your official name now becomes X, son of Y, of the *deme* Z. It is, in other words, the *phratries* and the *demes*, not the state, that confer citizenship and manage the citizen roster.

You're now a member of a city-state, a *deme*, and a *phratry*. Anything else? Yes, you're the member of a tribe – one of ten – into which the Athenian citizen body is divided. The ten tribes were established by a politician called Cleisthenes towards the end of the sixth century, so they're not particularly venerable. In fact, they're highly artificial. But they form the basis for all administrative divisions among the citizens. Athenians fight alongside other members of their tribe, sit beside them in the theatre, and serve alongside them in the Council of 500. You'll need to be literate to function fully as a citizen. You'll see public notices all over the place, including inscriptions recording decisions of the Assembly.

A woman is not a citizen in the same sense as a man. A daughter does not undergo the same scrutiny as a son, even though it is essential

Inscription.

that she, too, is the legitimate offspring of Athenian parents for her to be recognised as Athenian. How that fact is determined is a mystery. A woman doesn't belong to a *phratry* either, though if she's aristocratic, she will belong to a *genos,* or noble kin group. Only a minority of Athenians belong to a *genos*. Such groups are important in the political arena, to which we turn next.

The political arena

Participation in politics is expected of every citizen, irrespective of age. In the speech that he delivered in honour of the soldiers who died in the first year of the Peloponnesian War, Pericles remarked, 'We regard the man who takes no part in politics not as somebody who minds his own business but as good for nothing.' 'Good for nothing' says much about the opprobrium that attaches to those who attempt to duck the heavy demands of citizenship.

As an adult Athenian male you are permitted, or rather expected, to attend the Assembly and to vote on every issue under debate. Meetings of the Assembly take place four times a month, though we hear of one extraordinary meeting that was called at a moment's notice. They are held in the open air on the Pnyx, a low hill southwest of the Acropolis. In earlier times the Assembly met in the Agora but the population grew too large to be accommodated there.

Though the agenda of the Assembly is decided by the Council of 500, any citizen is entitled to bring forward a subject for discussion. The 500 councillors are annually appointed by lot. In theory, the head of the Athenian state is the *epistatês*, meaning literally 'the man who stands over', i.e. the overseer. But the *epistatês* is only in office for one day, so it's a purely ceremonial job. The most important officers of state are the *archons*, or magistrates, also annually appointed by lot. They include: the eponymous *archon*, who gives his name to the year, and who, among other duties, looks after the affairs involving metics; the king *archon*, who is in charge of religious observance; six other *archons* who are in charge of the courts and who decide which plays should be subsidised for performance at the dramatic festivals; and an *archon* known as the *polemarchos* (literal meaning 'war magistrate'), who is the nominal head of the army.

However, it isn't actually the *polemarchos* but the ten *stratêgoi*, or generals, who conduct military campaigns. The *stratêgoi* are among the very few officials who are elected by a popular vote. Whereas any Athenian is assumed to be as good as any other at handling routine state business, someone placed in charge of a military campaign is expected and required to have expertise and experience.

Once a year the *Dêmos,* the People, are asked if they want to hold an *ostrakismos* or ostracism. If they vote in the affirmative, every citizen will subsequently write the name of the prominent individual whom he wants to send into exile for ten years on an *ostrakon*, i.e. a piece of broken pottery. Broken pottery is the most readily available writing material. This is the origin of our word 'ostracism'; literally 'a vote that is recorded on a potsherd'. This expedient is evoked when two politicians are constantly locking horns and producing a stalemate. An ostracism breaks this impasse by eliminating one of them from the political arena. It isn't a punishment as such, but a kind of negative popularity contest.

Beliefs and Rituals

How to deal with death

What will strike you immediately on arrival in Athens is that death is ever-present and highly visible. Many people today rarely see a dead body, whereas you will regularly see death, both in the home and in the street, since corpses are displayed to public view on their way to burial. You also stand a much higher likelihood of being struck down by illness or accident or as a result of hostilities, than you do in our world. Similarly, the odds of your losing a parent, a sibling, or a close friend in childhood or adolescence are much higher than in our society. Will this affect your emotional attachment to those closest to you? Probably not, but I can't guarantee it. Herodotus praised the Persian practice of safeguarding fathers from having close contact with their sons until they had survived their early years, on the grounds that this spared the fathers from grieving should they die. This suggests that Greek fathers *did* form close attachments to their young children and that Persian fathers would have done so too, if permitted.

Women are at grave risk when giving birth. Their anxiety, and that of their families, is evident from the strenuous efforts they make to appease the goddess Artemis both before and during childbirth, since she is a virgin who is hostile to sexual congress.

As there are no hospitals, no old people's homes, and no hospices, deaths occur either on the battlefield or, in the vast majority of cases, in the home. There are no undertakers as such, though you can hire 'ladder carriers' to bear the body to the place of interment. It is the duty of the family – women primarily – to prepare the dead for burial. This they do by washing the body and placing it on a couch or a trestle table inside the house.

This ceremony is known as the *prothesis* or 'laying out' of the body. The room in which it takes place is festooned with swags of flowers and reeks with scent. People of all ages, including small children, attend, moaning, wailing and crying. It is customary to touch, fondle and kiss the corpse. Some mourners even fall into ecstasies of grief, tearing their hair and striking their breasts. Many do so in the belief that it gives the dead pleasure. At Patroclus' funeral in the *Iliad* Homer tells us that mourners wail 'using Patroclus as an excuse', meaning they are actually grieving for other lost loved ones. There's nothing wrong with remembering other dead at a moment like this.

At the *prothesis* the corpse is covered in a white shroud with the face exposed. She or he often wears a crown of gold leaf. A linen strap is tied around the chin to prevent the jaw from sagging and an obol is placed between the lips. You need to give the dead an obol to pay Charon, the ferryman of the dead. It's a paltry sum but if Charon doesn't receive his fare, the dead won't be able to enter Hades. Instead they will be forced to wander up and down the banks of the River Styx, which surrounds Hades, for hundreds of years. Such a condition is thought to be a fate worse than death.

Solon, whom I've mentioned, decreed that the *prothesis* can last only a day and that the body must be transported to the place of burial before

Mourners surrounding a corpse.

dawn the next day. Previously there had been no limit to the grieving period. Solon's intention was to prevent the survivors from exploiting a funeral for political effect by drawing attention to their wealth, prominence and political clout.

The body is conveyed to the place of burial in a cart, perhaps hired specially for the purpose. Burial is not permitted inside the city walls for fear of causing pollution or *miasma*. Pollution is the reason why those who come into contact with a corpse are debarred from entering sanctuaries and other public places for a month or more afterwards.

Many dead are buried alongside roads outside the city gates – another way in which death is highly visible. This is why funerary monuments often bear inscriptions that address the passer-by, seeking her or his attention and perhaps supplying a brief bio. In Athens, the most prestigious burial ground is the Ceramicus. As you'll recall, the Ceramicus lies outside the city wall on its west side. Both sides of the roads that run through it are lined with funerary monuments. Imposing retaining walls, some as many as 5m in height, identify the most prestigious family plots, just as mausolea do in our culture.

Both inhumation and cremation are practised. The only distinction seems to be that, owing to the costliness of wood, only the wealthy can afford to cremate. It is de rigueur to send your dead on their way with grave gifts. The most popular grave gift is a painted pot. The commonest vase used for this purpose is a *lêkythos*, a small container for olive oil up to 45cm high. *Lêkythoi* are often decorated with scenes depicting mourners bringing gifts to the dead and revering the funerary monument. They are painted against a white background, often in an impressionistic style.

No burial service is performed at the grave. If prayers are delivered, we know nothing of them. The reason for the absence of religious ritual is that the gods scrupulously avoid the dying and the dead for fear they will become

Lêkythos or olive oil container depicting a tomb.

85

polluted. That's why priests aren't allowed to enter a house of mourning, be present at a *prothesis*, or attend an interment.

Don't forget to make a will; if you're a man. Women can't make a will because they don't own property. Making a will is pretty straightforward because, as we've seen, the law requires you to leave your estate exclusively to your son or sons. If you don't have any offspring, adopted or otherwise, you are free to dispose of your estate to whomever you wish. That's so long as your judgement hasn't been impaired by 'either madness or senility or drugs or disease or' – get this one – by 'a woman's persuasion,' as a law quoted by Demosthenes states. It's no surprise to learn that the Athenians don't trust women when it comes to finances, given the low opinion they hold of their trustworthiness and intelligence. In *Laws*, Plato, who became more repressive and intolerant as he aged, describes women as 'the naturally more furtive and secretive sex.'

I'd like to take this opportunity briefly to point out that not all Greek men hold a low opinion of women's character, however. Sophocles' portrait of Antigone shows a woman who is fully equal to a man, and there are many other female characters who are no less capable and forceful.

Interpreting signs from the gods

Interpreting signs from the gods runs in the family. If your father is a seer, it's likely you'll become one too. Seers regard themselves as descended from Apollo, the patron god of seercraft. It's a highly skilled profession, requiring the interpretation of oracular utterances. An oracle contains hidden knowledge sent from the divine world to the human. Most oracles are obscure and some are deliberately misleading, like the one Croesus, king of Lydia, received, which informed him that if he attacked Persia, he'd destroy a great empire. He forgot to ask whose empire the god meant and destroyed his own.

Sticking with Persia, when Xerxes was preparing to launch his expedition against Greece, the Athenians received an oracle from Delphi instructing them to 'trust the wooden wall'. The professional seers took this to be a reference to the ropey old wooden fence surrounding the Acropolis. As a result a lot of pious Athenians who tried to defend it were massacred by the Persians.

What Apollo really meant by 'wooden wall' was the Athenian fleet, because a wooden wall is a metaphor for a ship. Any idiot should have been able to work that out, because the Persian army was far superior to the Athenian, and there was no hope that a literal wooden wall would keep the invaders out. The Persians burned down the temples on the Acropolis and cut down the olive tree that grows up there, sacred to Athena. Miraculously, however, it put up a new shoot next day.

It was Themistocles who discovered the true meaning of the phrase 'wooden wall'. Under his direction, the Athenians fought the Persians at sea and won an astounding naval victory.

You certainly need to use your intelligence when interpreting an oracle. It's not as if Apollo hands out answers to you on a plate. Not for nothing does the inscription on the wall around the sanctuary at Delphi read, 'Know yourself'. The point is that it's pointless to have foresight if you don't have insight to go with it. Think of the story of Oedipus. When he was born, Apollo told his parents that he was fated to kill his father and marry his mother. Naturally they were terrified at the thought of raising a sociopathic monster, so they ordered a servant to abandon the baby in a deserted spot with nails driven through its ankles so that it would have zero chance of survival. But the servant took pity on the infant and handed it over to a nomadic shepherd, who gave it to the king and queen of Corinth, Polybus and Merope, and they adopted the infant because they were childless.

When Oedipus grew up, some drunk told him he wasn't the son of the king and queen, so he went to Delphi to ask Apollo who his real parents were. Apollo just repeated the original prophecy. Still assuming that Polybus and Merope were his parents, Oedipus took the precaution of giving Corinth a wide berth in the belief that he could escape his destiny. On the road, he encountered an old man and his servants blocking his path. He killed the old man and all but one of his servants and headed on his way, where, he found his way blocked by the Sphinx, a creature with the head of a human and the body of a lion, which asked him what goes on four legs in the morning, two in the afternoon, three in the evening. Answer: man, because he crawls on all fours as an infant and leans on a stick

Oedipus and the Sphinx in conversation.

when he grows old. Oedipus gave the correct answer and arrived in Thebes, where, lo and behold, the queen had been recently widowed. He didn't discover the truth until a plague broke out, which he had caused because he was a polluted murderer.

Seers are always in high demand when there's a crisis. Before the Peloponnesian War broke out, everyone wanted to know how long it would last, who would win, what would happen to their family, and so on. When Pericles implemented his plan to evacuate everyone living in the countryside, a number of seers produced an oracle that said under no condition should anyone ever occupy the vacant land around the base of the Acropolis. Well, the vacant land *was* occupied and that is why a terrible plague broke out a few months later. Ignoring an oracle is just asking for trouble. And when a seer gives the correct interpretation of an oracle as important as that one was, everyone sits up and takes notice and wants his advice.

Though seers only address the Assembly as ordinary citizens, they still have a lot of clout. Many generals keep a seer on hand when they're on a campaign to help them interpret the entrails of a sacrificial victim or some other sign sent by the gods. Victory is as much the result of interpreting the will of the gods as it is of military strategy and tactics.

Too much dependency on signs from the gods can land you in a terrible mess, however. A few years after your arrival in ancient Greece, the Athenians will appoint three generals to undertake the expedition to Sicily. The most senior will be Nicias. Nicias isn't exactly a livewire but he's a trusted pair of hands. He'll be accompanied by two other generals, Lamachus and Alcibiades. However, Lamachus will die of disease shortly after arrival and Alcibiades will desert to Sparta, so Nicias will be left in sole command. That's extremely unfortunate, to say the least, because he was opposed to the expedition in the first place. He's very religious and believes strongly in signs from the gods.

It's his unwavering belief in portents from the gods that will ultimately prove his undoing; with catastrophic consequences for his entire army. After failing to take Syracuse, the most powerful *polis* in Sicily, Nicias will delay his retreat for twenty-seven days due to an eclipse of the moon, which his seer interprets as a sign to stay put. In the interval the Syracusans will enclose the mouth of their harbour in order to blockade the Athenian fleet. When Nicias finally orders a retreat, he'll have no option but to try to evacuate by land. By this point his men will be so weakened by disease and exhaustion that they won't be able to put up any resistance. This is the fate that will be awaiting Athens, a few years after your arrival.

What to expect in the Afterlife

The Greeks believe that virtually everyone ends up in the same place, namely Hades, the kingdom of the dead, which is ruled by its namesake Hades, otherwise known as Pluto, and his wife Persephone. To enter Hades, you will have to cross the River Styx. Charon, the boatman, will ferry you across for a fee, as mentioned.

Hades is dark, damp, and draughty. 'Inspissated' is the word that best captures the atmosphere. Unless you happen to be a student of Plato, which is highly unlikely, since he'll only be 15-years old when you arrive and even Plato can't have been that precocious, you won't have to worry about a post mortem judgement. There's nothing equivalent to Heaven for the good people or Hell for the bad people; unless you win immortal glory as a warrior, in which case you'll be wafted away either to Elysium or the Isles of the Blest, where life is a breeze, or unless you have done something really outrageous to offend the gods, in which case you'll end up in Tartarus, a place of torment way below Hades. One of its denizens is Tantalus, who served his son, Pelops, to the gods in a casserole in the belief that they were too stupid to realise that they would be eating human flesh. Demeter exposed the affront by identifying a human shoulder bone. Hence his punishment, by being perpetually 'tantalised' with the promise of grapes and water that are always receding from his reach.

A large number of Greeks undergo initiation into what are known as the Mysteries, viz. ritual activities from which the general public are excluded. Our word 'mystery' comes from the Greek *mustês*, meaning 'initiate'. They undergo initiation in the belief that they will lead a blessed existence in Hades. However, what precisely these Mysteries consist of and what blessedness means in this context, is, so to speak, a complete mystery. The most famous of these Mysteries are celebrated at Eleusis on the west coast of Attica. The Eleusinian Mysteries attract celebrants from all over the Greek world. Their popularity will later present a severe threat to the early Christians, who will vandalise the sanctuary on the specious grounds that it served as a cover for sexual debauchery.

The dead down in Hades remain dependent on the living and are forever pitifully eager for their attention. Well, who *doesn't* like attention? Who wants to be forgotten? That's why relatives pay regular visits to their graves with food, drink and other offerings. In fact, the ties between the living and the dead remain very much alive. The Athenians and probably other Greeks believe you will be reunited with your loved ones, though what you will do together for all eternity in that murky darkness is anyone's guess. But family ties endure and that is some crumb of comfort for being a shade, though you'll also have to be prepared to bump into your enemies. That's what happens to Odysseus when he descends to the Underworld; he encounters Ajax, his defeated rival in the competition for the gold armour of Achilles. Ajax refuses to acknowledge Odysseus because he is still eaten up with undying rancour. He has failed to 'move on', as we say. And what about ex-husbands and ex-wives? They'll be there awaiting your arrival as well.

The high incidence of death among the young and the brevity of human life casts a heavy pall over Greek society. No grave monument is more poignant than that in the shape of a giant marble vase known as a *loutrophoros*, which is filled with sacred water for a bride and groom to bathe in on their wedding day. Monuments of this sort mark the graves of young men and women who attained the age of marriage but who died unwed.

The sort of gods you're going to believe in

I've already talked quite a bit about religion because, whatever your belief, or lack of belief right now, you're going to find yourself living in a

90

world that is subject to divine intervention at any moment: when you go on a sea voyage, when you fight in battle, when you start drinking, when your ardour is aroused by someone to whom you are attracted, when you work in a hard hat area without a hard hat, when you give birth, when you plant seeds in the ground, and so on. All these activities and many others may be aided or thwarted by the gods. It is, therefore, vital to *get the gods on your side.*

The Greeks are extremely religious, even though they don't actually have a word for 'religion'. And though they devote a great deal of energy and resources to placating their gods and securing their goodwill, you could hardly describe them as religious in our sense of the word. Nor is their religion expected to promote goodness.

Our word 'atheist', which comes from their adjective *atheos*, primarily means someone who is godless, i.e. someone who pays no attention to the gods. There is no word in the Greek language to differentiate an atheist from someone who is godless. Some Greeks *do* have doubts about the gods, however. When in Aristophanes' *Clouds* Socrates, whose character is based only loosely on the philosopher, is asked if he believes in Zeus, he replies 'Zeus? Don't talk rubbish. He definitely doesn't exist.'

Bear in mind, though, that this is in a comic context. As in any religious system, not everyone is singing from the same hymn sheet, so to speak. Socrates in the dialogues of Plato occasionally invokes what he calls 'the god'. Very possibly he is moving towards a belief in only one god.

Within Attica alone, there are some 2,000 gods and goddesses, all clamouring for your attention. You can't possibly worship even a fraction of them, of course. One of the basic problems that you'll have to face, therefore, is that you won't

Socrates.

necessarily know which deity to placate before, say, undertaking a hazardous enterprise, or which to thank afterwards. To cover their bases, as the Americans say, the Athenians have set up an altar to the Unknown God in the Agora. It's a kind of insurance policy, in case they've left one out.

The gods spend most of their time up on Mount Olympus, just occasionally bothering themselves with the fate of human beings. Being anthropomorphic, they're endowed with all our negative emotions, as well as with all our body parts. This means they can be extremely mean-spirited, greedy, vindictive, resentful, jealous, deceitful, cantankerous, lustful and avaricious. The Greeks reckon that the gods do exactly what humans *would* do if only they had the same opportunity and power. Rarely do they demonstrate any compassion or generous impulse, they certainly don't do anything for nothing, and though erotic desire is certainly in their vocabulary, they seem to know very little about love.

I have to confess, however, that most of what we know about the gods comes from poetry, principally Homer and the tragedians. Homer paints an extremely unflattering picture of them, though the gods in Euripides' dramas are hardly less cynical and self-interested. Once you immerse yourself in ancient Greek culture, you may find out that the gods aren't quite as bad as the poets paint them. In their defence, and to their infinite credit, they can take a joke against themselves, and this distinguishes them from the gods in any other religious system (with which I am familiar). Dionysus, for instance, is expected to have a good old laugh at the City Dionysia when his on-stage character, who is a bit of a coward, has a sudden attack of diarrhea in Aristophanes' *Frogs*.

The main difference between humans and gods is that the latter are physically perfect, incredibly strong, and both ageless and deathless. Even Zeus doesn't have it entirely his own way, however. Though he's the number one god, he has to mind his p's and q's when it comes to his wife Hera. In the *Iliad* she causes him to fall into a post-coital slumber and manages to alter, albeit temporarily, the course of the Trojan War. Her husband's predilection for serial hanky panky is especially galling to her, since she's the goddess of marriage. To evade detection he often assumes a disguise, as when he seduces Europa in the form of a bull.

Olympianism speaks of a world where elemental forces are always raging, whether out in the world at large or deep inside your head and heart. Aphrodite can cause you intense pleasure or intense pain, whether

Zeus disguised as a bull abducting Europa.

or not your love is requited. Poseidon can cause placid sailing conditions or a destructive tempest. Dionysus can cause you to forget your cares or make you run riot. The turmoil in our world thus makes perfect sense, because it is largely due to the fact that the gods are constantly at loggerheads with one another.

No deity, however, is simply good or bad. From an ethical standpoint, they are amoral. They are capable of making both good *and* bad things happen. Generally, they choose to do good or bad according to their own self-interest. 'How will they benefit from helping me?' is the question you therefore have to ask yourself when you're eliciting their support. In other words, don't bother to contact them unless you've got something to give them. There's a revealing inscription on a bronze figurine. It reads: 'From Mantiklos to Apollo, who shoots a long distance with his bow. Give me something nice in return.' Mantiklos couldn't have put it more plainly than that.

There are also a number of deities, mostly female, who are perceived as personifications. They include Justice, Peace, Memory, Fortune, Lawfulness, the Seasons, the Graces, and so on. Their number will increase as time passes.

The Greeks also acknowledge as supernatural deities associated with the earth and the Underworld, and human beings who have been accorded heroic status. Among the so-called chthonic or earth deities are the Furies, whom I mentioned earlier. Heroes can be summoned by a blood sacrifice in the vicinity of their tomb.

Bear in mind that you can't expect to have a personal relationship with any god as, for instance, a Christian can with Jesus. True, Odysseus has a personal relationship with Athena – basically because they're both very tricky – but that is very much the exception that proves the rule, and anyway he's a character in fiction. If you do try to develop a personal relationship with a deity, it may well end badly. This is what happens to Hippolytus in Euripides' play of that name – the young man accused of rape by his stepmother, whom I mentioned before. Hippolytus develops an exclusive relationship with Artemis because he's not interested in sex and is destroyed by her rival Aphrodite, who is incensed at being ignored.

One of the charges against Socrates at his trial will be that he communicated with an unnamed personal deity, which he calls his *daimonion* or 'little divine spirit'. '*Daimonion*' gives us our word 'demon', which is ironic to say the least, because the best translation of the word as employed by Socrates is 'conscience'. The Athenians become outraged because no one has the right to claim an exclusive relationship with a god, not even with a little divine spirit.

How to get the gods on your side

There are essentially two ways to invoke the favour of a deity: either by making a votive dedication to the one whose goodwill you are enlisting, or by performing a sacrifice or libation. Such actions must

Man performing sacrifice.

be accompanied by prayer. Where appropriate, remind the deity of any previous gifts you have given or sacrifices you have performed. That will help grab their attention. Always remember that they've got a lot of better things to do than attend to the gripes of wretched mortals.

A votive dedication is anything of value. For instance, it can take the form of a small terracotta figurine in the image of the deity, which you deposit in the sanctuary or inside the temple. The chances are, however, that unless it's rather special it won't do much good. It's best if you give something precious; a bronze figurine, say, like that of Mantiklos, or, better still, a life-size statue. If you're an aristocrat, you might commission a hymn and have it sung by a choir.

A sacrificial victim, might offer a sheep, a goat or a pig; or better, several sheep, etc. The more victims the merrier in fact. If worse comes to worst, offer a chicken or some produce from your garden, such as fruit or vegetables. The biggest sacrifices take place at festivals held in honour of the state deities, when hundreds of animals are slain. These are financed out of public funds and closely regulated. As a libation, make an offering of wine, honey or milk; or all three combined. The same principle obtains with sacrifices and libations as it does with dedications: the more generous you are, the more likely the deity will heed your prayer.

Every god has a special day in the calendar devoted to her or him. On the birthday of Athena, the state sacrifices 300 head of oxen. Her birthday month is *Hekatombaion*, which means literally 'the 100-sacrifice event'. Sometimes only a part of the victim, sometimes the whole of it, is burned. The Greek word that gives us 'holocaust' means literally the burning of an entire victim. Gods don't actually devour the meat, but they relish the savoury smoke that rises up to Mount Olympus. In fact, *thuein*, the Greek word for 'to sacrifice', means literally 'to make smoke'.

Competitions, known as the Panathenaic or 'All-Athenian' games, are also held on the occasion of Athena's birthday. The prize is an amphora, a large two-handled jug filled with olive oil, which is Athens' staple export. Each amphora depicts the goddess brandishing her spear on one side and the athletic event for which the prize has been awarded on the other.

Aside from praying, making dedications and offering sacrifices, you should act piously. Piety is extremely difficult to define. In Plato's dialogue of the same name, Euthyphro, who claims to be a religious expert, offers several definitions, but Socrates shoots down each of them in turn. In the course of his interrogation, he raises a question that is fundamental to every religious system: is an action good because the god loves it or does the god love it because it is good? Know the answer?

The most visible symbol of worship is the temple, of which the supreme example in Athens is the Parthenon, erected in honour of Athena Parthenos. The majority of sanctuaries, however, consist merely of a sacred space demarcated with a mudbrick wall and an altar made out of roughly hewn stones or terracotta. An altar, in fact, is the only feature that is needed for worship, though few have survived owing to their generally rough and ready method of construction. The most grandiloquent example is the altar of Zeus from Pergamum, near Izmir, in modern-day Turkey, which is today housed in the Altes Museum on Museum Island in Berlin. It's an outstanding example of Hellenistic art, i.e. art belonging to the period after the death of Alexander the Great. Because of its colossal size and appearance, you might easily mistake it for a temple.

The worship of the gods is conducted out in the open. No religious observance takes place inside a temple, which is used solely for displaying the cult statue and storing dedications and implements that are used for cultic purposes. Most of the year the temple is closed. It's only open when the deity is staying over, at which time it serves as her or his temporary residence.

Sanctuaries have to be spotlessly clean because the gods will only visit a sanctuary if it's completely pure. Purity is vital to their well-being. That's why they don't have anything to do with the dying or the dead, since death is a source of pollution. Pollution is very nasty stuff, as we've seen already, and the last thing you want is for it to seep into a sanctuary. That's why you'll find a basin of purified water at the entrance, just as you do at the entrance to a church.

Should you become polluted, say by contact with the dead or with a murderer, the best way to purify yourself is with pig's blood. Murder is the most powerful cause of pollution. You can become polluted just by being in the presence of a murderer. That's sometimes the reason why tempests occur. If there's a murderer on board a ship, the gods may choose to sink the ship just to punish him. Tough luck if you happen to be on board as well. The gods won't give a damn about you. You'll just be collateral damage.

Religious observance isn't limited to sanctuaries. Every morning the head of the household invokes the goodwill of the deities who protect his home. The most important of these deities is Hestia, goddess of the hearth. Every household has a hearth, which symbolically represents its heart: the English words 'heart' and 'hearth' are related linguistically. Other household deities include Zeus Ktesios (Of property) and Zeus Herkeios (Of the boundary). It is Zeus Herkeios who guards your house against trespassers. Household deities appreciate even a modest offering of fruit and nuts, though on special occasions you'll want to offer them something more.

What happens at a religious festival

Most religious festivals are small affairs, in which only a small section of the citizen body participate. However, the festivals held in honour of major deities, such as Athena and Dionysus, are attended by thousands and no expense is spared. Public business will be suspended, the courts will be closed, and your participation will be expected. That's partly why Socrates fell foul of the democracy. One of the charges brought against him was 'not acknowledging the gods whom the state acknowledges'. In other words, he didn't turn up. Turning up is important. The gods, as well as the state, expect it.

Every festival begins at dawn with a procession along a ceremonial way that ends up at the deity's shrine. The celebrating priest or priestess heads the procession, officiants and worshippers follow behind, and in the midst sacrificial victims shamble along.

When the procession reaches its destination, the sacrificial victims are herded into a pen and the priest or priestess, standing beside the altar, delivers a prayer while looking up at the sky with outstretched arms. After the sacrifice has been performed, officiants roast the vital organs on spits and boil the rest of the meat in cauldrons, taking care not to slip in the pool of blood at their feet. When the meat has been cooked, they distribute it among the worshippers, giving the priest and other dignitaries a larger share than the rest.

Why you might want to consult an oracle

The Greeks believe that their gods regularly send signs intended to warn them of the outcome of their actions, so it's a good idea to consult an oracle whenever you're faced with a big decision. The most important oracular sanctuary is that of Apollo at Delphi. Delphi is the navel of the earth. We know that for a fact because Zeus, in order to locate the centre spot, released two eagles who met at a fissure in the rocks above Delphi. The sanctuary isn't located on a major highway, so to get there you'll either have to trek along a cart track or sail to a nearby port and hike up a hill. Be prepared to wait in line for a considerable length of time. Apollo's sanctuary is only in session for a few days every year and there's bound to be a long queue of petitioners.

19th century etching
of Delphi.

Exactly what happens at an oracular consultation is unknown. All we know for certain is that you will put your question to the god through a priestess who is called the Pythia. She's so named because Apollo's cult title is *Pythios*. The god was given this title because he killed a python when he first arrived at Delphi. The Pythia, a kind of female medium, will give you Apollo's response. Quite likely what she utters will be unfathomable, in which case an interpreter will promptly step forward and, no doubt for a fee, explain its meaning in plain Greek. Even then you will need to study it carefully and not jump to rash conclusions. Not for nothing are the words 'Know yourself' inscribed on the retaining wall of the sanctuary. Knowledge of the future is not much use without self-knowledge.

Delphi today.

Professional seers equipped with prophecies are also plentiful throughout the Greek world, so if you can't make it to Delphi for some reason, you can always engage the services of a seer in Athens. We'll meet a seer later.

Consulting an oracle or a seer isn't the only way of gaining insight into the future. Meteorological phenomena such as eclipses and flights of birds are other tried and tested methods. Even a sneeze at the right or wrong moment can be ominous. You'll soon learn that the gods are doing their best to assist you in your decision-making. You'll have no one but yourself to blame if you don't take their warnings seriously.

We think of the Greeks as a very rational people, and so they are in some ways. But they also believe – profoundly – that the human and divine worlds are intimately connected. That's not to say that you won't encounter the odd sceptic. When a speechwriter called Antiphon is asked to define prophecy, he replies, 'Speculation by a sensible man.' Admittedly this is the intelligentsia talking, but remember that the average Athenian has a pretty high IQ.

Relaxation and Entertainment

How to relax

I'm afraid I'm going to be talking mainly about what freeborn men get up to in this section. Freeborn women and slaves don't really have the chance to relax. Freeborn women have the household to look after. Slaves, when they're not working, grab what chance they can to sleep.

How you as an Athenian will fill your vacant hours will be entirely your own business. You're certainly not required to return home to your wife at the end of an exhausting day spent gossiping and chewing the cud in the Agora.

You may be tempted to visit a tavern or a brothel, though most are pretty seedy. You probably won't contract a sexually transmitted disease but you may well lose an eye in a brawl. So I recommend you give them a wide berth.

The only form of domestic entertainment is the symposium, which is held in the home, ideally in the *andrôn*, the 'men's room'. An *andrôn* is detectable in the archaeological record because it has an off-centre doorway to accommodate the couches that are placed alongside the walls. Reclining, not sitting, is de rigueur at a symposium. It's a tradition that derives from the east.

A symposium, like every gathering in the Greek world, is a religious event. It begins with prayers and it ends with a hymn to Apollo. You don't drink pure wine; that's the hallmark of barbarians and it leads to madness. Instead you drink wine diluted with water. A ratio of one part wine to three parts water is considered safe. One to one is very risky. The proportion of wine to water will be determined by the symposiarch, or 'master of the symposium', who is appointed before the drinking starts to set the tone of the proceedings.

Drinker reclining at a symposium.

This will be a suitable place to talk about homosexuality, since the symposium provides one of the principal outlets for homosexual activity. You've probably heard that homosexuality is condoned in Greek society. But there are strict limits. Firstly, there's a strong expectation that it will be between a younger and an older man; typically between a youth in his late-teens and a man in his late-twenties to early-thirties. Secondly, such a relationship isn't exclusively about sexual gratification. On the contrary, it's expected that the older man will perform the duties of a mentor. A symposium is the ideal venue for such a relationship to develop, in part because it's where ideas on a variety of topics are aired and where familiarity with literature and other forms of culture is assumed. Thirdly, the relationship between the two partners is generally short term because homosexuality is viewed as an episodic phenomenon, as I mentioned earlier. In other words, the Greeks don't acknowledge it as an orientation. In fact, if a man *does* devote his affections exclusively to males, he is likely to be ridiculed as an effeminate. And the fourth point to note is that there are very strict laws against pederasty. In Athens teachers are not permitted to be alone with their pupils in the dark.

We hear little about lesbianism, though that doesn't mean it doesn't exist. The poet Sappho, who lived on the island of Lesbos, which has given us our name for female homosexuality, certainly had lesbian tendencies. But she lived in the sixth century and there's little evidence for the practice in any later period. Perhaps it was a taboo subject and no one dared talk about it.

The tone of a symposium naturally depends on the occasion and the temperament of the drinkers. Plato in his dialogue the *Symposium* suggests a very sedate and philosophical affair, with the drinkers each giving a speech about love. But this is surely the exception rather than the rule. More likely there'll be flute girls and dancers galore and a lot of slap and tickle going on. You might find yourself playing a mindless game such as *kottabos*, which requires the drinkers to chuck the remaining drops of wine in their drinking cups at a target to see which of them can topple it over and make the loudest clatter. I dare say it's fun when you're tipsy. There's a proverb that says a lot about what goes on at the average symposium: 'I hate a symposiast with a good memory.' In other words, 'What happens in Vegas, stays in Vegas.'

Permission to attend a symposium is restricted to freeborn men and *hetairai*. If you're a wife or daughter, sister or mother, grandmother or aunt or niece, you won't be welcome. Bear in mind, however, that your husband will hardly be drinking with his buddies every evening. On one or two evenings a week he will probably grace you with his presence.

Going to the theatre

The Athenians invented drama and they've never had any rivals. Can you imagine what it would be like sitting through a play written by a Spartan? Very boring. The god of drama is Dionysus. Some Greeks wonder what Dionysus has to do with drama since he's the god of wine. An obvious explanation is that wine brings liberation and with it the ability to change one's identity.

Bust of Aeschylus.

Tragedians have to write a trilogy, i.e. three plays. Only one trilogy has survived. That's Aeschylus' *Oresteia*, which is based around the life of Orestes. If ever there was a case of familial dysfunction, this is it. In the first play, called *Agamemnon*, Clytemnestra and her lover murder her husband, Agamemnon, Orestes' father. In the second play, *Libation Bearers*, Orestes murders Clytemnestra in revenge but is driven mad by monstrous creatures known as the Furies, who take the side of his mother. In the third play, *Eumenides*, the Furies pursue Orestes to Delphi, where he seeks purification, and then to Athens, where he's acquitted of his crime in a law court that is set up under the supervision of Athena. The trilogy explains how the rule of law was established in Athens to halt an endless cycle of revenge killings.

Greek tragedy has many powerful female characters. One of the most memorable is Clytemnestra, who proves she's every bit as determined and ruthless as any man. She cold-bloodedly invites Agamemnon into the palace and offers to give him a bath just so that she can kill him when he's at his most vulnerable. She also kills his war-bride Cassandra, whom he has the audacity to bring home and flaunt in her face. I'm sure you'll discover equally strong-willed women in Athens – women who have inspired the dramatists to create such portraits.

The audience doesn't actually see Agamemnon or Cassandra being murdered – violent acts are never performed on stage – but it does hear Agamemnon's blood-curdling scream. When at the first production the actor playing Clytemnestra emerged from the building that represents the palace and displayed her or rather his bloody hand, the audience gasped in horror. They gasped again watching the last play in the trilogy when the Furies appeared with snakes in their hair, flecks of blood around their mouths, and puss oozing out of their eyes. Great stuff!

Everything goes out of fashion eventually, of course. When Aeschylus died, Sophocles became all the rage, and now Euripides' star is rising. Lots of Athenians think Euripides has gone too far. They say he doesn't have any respect for the gods and presents them in a poor light. That's true, but he was hardly the first dramatist to do that. Aeschylus didn't show the gods in the best possible light and nor did Sophocles.

Each tragedian also writes a satyr play, intended perhaps as a reward to the audience for having sat through all that misery. Satyrs are half-human and half-goat creatures, who enjoy boozing and harassing women. They'd all be locked up in jail today for non-consensual sex.

In addition to tragedy, there's also comedy. The only comic plays that have survived from this period are by Aristophanes. Comedies, unlike tragedies, are based on current events. In *Acharnians* a farmer negotiates a private peace with the Spartans. In *Lysistrata* all the women go on a sex strike to end the Peloponnesian War. In *Clouds* the playwright makes fun of all the claptrap that philosophers spout and the exorbitant fees they charge for their services.

Drama began under the auspices of a shadowy figure called Thespis. At that time there was only a single actor plus the chorus. This meant that you couldn't have a real dialogue because the actor only interacted with the chorus. It was Aeschylus who introduced the second actor and Sophocles who introduced the third, with the result that a real conversation between two or three people became possible.

Three speaking actors will remain the limit throughout antiquity. This means that each actor usually plays two or even three parts. He has to be skilled at changing character at a moment's notice. He can only do this because he wears a mask or rather several masks. Since he plays both men and women, he has to have a wide vocal range. Every actor begins his career at the bottom rung of the ladder as a tritagonist. Then he graduates to becoming a deuteragonist, and finally, if he's talented enough, he becomes a protagonist, which means he gets the lead role.

Actors don't get paid, but they do gain a lot of kudos from appearing on stage. It's obviously a huge privilege to bring to life the characters whom the playwrights have imagined at a festival devoted to Dionysus, but it's also a challenge to keep the audience's attention, with people eating and drinking throughout the performance. If the audience thinks the actors are bad, they'll pelt them with nuts and fruit.

When all three tragedians or all three comic playwrights have had their plays performed, ten judges known as *kritai*, from which our word 'critic' comes, cast their votes to determine who will be awarded first, second and third prize. You don't need any previous experience or background to qualify to be a judge. Any Athenian can do the job, just as any Athenian can vote on matters of state. For that reason the *kritai* are appointed by lot.

The first prize is awarded – technically – not to the dramatist but to the *chorêgos,* the rich Athenian who footed the bill for all the expenses incurred by the production. However, it's hard to imagine that the quality of the writing doesn't play some part in the judges' verdict. Well, to be fair, it isn't exclusively the judges who make the choice because only five of the ten votes cast are actually drawn from the jar in which they're placed. This means that Dionysus gets to vote as well.

One of the biggest expenses that the *chorêgos* faces is the costumes that the choruses wear: four in the case of a tragic production; just one in the case of a comic production. The costumes of comic choruses are often very fanciful, as we know from the titles of the plays – *Wasps, Frogs, Clouds, Birds,* etc. – and very costly to produce.

How to keep fit

Men keep fit by frequenting a gymnasium, often spending several hours there. We don't hear of a lower age limit for entry to a gymnasium, but it's likely that boys are debarred for safety reasons. We don't know whether metics are allowed to patronize them either. 'Gymnasium' means literally 'a place of nakedness', since Greeks exercise naked. Indeed it is a point of pride that they condone male nakedness. In years to come this will put them at serious odds with Jewish practice and Jewish religion, since Jews keep their bodies covered in the sight of God; that and the fact that the Greeks don't practise circumcision, whose effect they find aesthetically unappealing.

(An aside: when you arrive in Athens in 420 there won't be any Jewish people living in Athens. The two cultures haven't met yet. Greek influence on Jewish culture will be profound in the Hellenistic period, however, notwithstanding their profound differences.)

You can't shower or bath at a gymnasium – the Greeks aren't the Romans – and showers haven't been invented yet, but since gymnasia are often located beside rivers, you'll be able to take a dip afterwards. Once you've finished exercising, you can clean away the dirt and perspiration by applying olive oil to your body and scraping your skin with a bronze instrument with a curved blade known as a strigil. Strigils are highly personal items and are often placed in the grave with their owners.

Greeks place a very high importance on physical fitness, not least because the security of the state depends on the speed, agility, discipline and tenacity of its warriors. Gymnasia aren't only places to exercise, however. They're also what we would call social spaces. It's not accidental that some have already become the haunts of philosophers. In the fourth century, two will even become homes to philosophical schools. One will be Plato's Academy, established in the grove of the hero Academos, from which our word 'academic' derives. Another will be Aristotle's Lyceum, which will also have a gymnasium attached to it. 'Lyceum' derives from Apollo Lykeios, who has a sanctuary in its grounds. The teaching facilities of both schools will be added later.

There's no equivalent to a gymnasium for women. Only in Sparta do we hear of girls exercising.

Bust of Plato.

Public entertainment

In the speech that he delivers over the war dead at the beginning of the Peloponnesian War, Pericles contrasts the many days for relaxation that the Athenians enjoy with the few that are available to the Spartans. 'All work and no play makes Jack a dull boy' could have been coined by the Athenians. Though these days off are all religious occasions of high solemnity, they're also opportunities to mingle, enjoy free meat at a sacrifice, and perhaps spectate at athletic and musical competitions.

Two of the most important festivals are the City Dionysia and the Lenaea, at which theatrical performances take place. I've already talked about drama, but I want to say more, as it's so vital to Athenian society. I estimate that at least 1,500 individuals are involved in theatrical productions each year. Almost all of these are men, though I suspect that women make the costumes.

I'll begin with tragedy. Only a few tragedies are actually set in Athens. A far larger percentage are based on events that occurred during the Trojan War and its aftermath. Tragedy deals with subjects that have perennial importance, such as enmity within the family or conflicts between individual and state. Though they set their plays in the distant past, therefore, tragedians may be responding to some recent event of which we have no knowledge.

Comedies by contrast are set in contemporary Athens, many of them freighted with a political message. Roughly in the middle of a comic play the chorus might even step out of its role and lecture the audience – not too strong a word – on some issue of urgent political concern (thus breaking what we call the 'fourth wall'). Comic dramatists frequently lampoon demagogues and philosophers, treating the former as slimeballs, the latter as airheads. A playwright called Eupolis, only fragments of whose plays survive, writes, 'I hate blabbermouths like Socrates. They're full of ideas but they don't concern themselves about where their next meal is coming from.' I have to say the fellow has a point.

The audience sits in a cone-shaped auditorium, known as the *theatron*, 'a place for seeing', which has been carved, almost literally, out of the Acropolis on its south side. Because of its shape, its acoustics are as near to perfection as they can be. Even if you're sitting right at the back, you can literally hear a pin drop. It's divided into ten wedges with steps in between. Each wedge is allocated to a specific tribe, of which there

The theatre at Epidaurus.

are ten, as you'll recall. This makes spectating an intensely civic, as well as religious experience.

We don't know whether women and children are permitted to attend the theatre. You'll have to report back when you return to the modern world, assuming you choose to do so.

The performance begins as soon as the sun comes up. It probably lasts about five to six hours, so you'll need to concentrate hard. I advise you to wrap up warmly for the Lenaea festival, which is held in late February or early March.

The action takes place in a large circle known as the *orchêstra,* whose literal meaning is 'dancing place'. Its name derives from the fact that the chorus, which occupies it throughout the play, dances while it sings. A low building, known as the *skênê* gives us our word 'scenery'. It provides a kind of backcloth and is where the actors change costume. It's commonly painted to resemble a palace or temple.

Most plays receive only a single performance, so if you miss the first performance, say, of Euripides' *Trojan Women,* which will be performed at the City Dionysia a few months after you arrive, you might have to wait two thousand five hundred years before you can see it again. Well, I'm exaggerating ever so slightly. Several demes have theatres which stage revivals at a local festival known as the Rural Dionysia, though these are amateur affairs by comparison with the state-sponsored productions. Anyway, the number of days that you can attend the theatre each year in Athens will be strictly limited. There's nothing equivalent to a run in the West End or on Broadway, where you can pick which day suits you best.

Athens is one of the very few places where plays are performed in the Classical period. In the succeeding Hellenistic period theatres will pop up everywhere and revivals of dramas by Aeschylus, Sophocles and Euripides will become commonplace. Thousands of new plays will also continue to be cranked out for hundreds of years. It will be a huge waste of effort, however, because of all these nothing except fragments will survive, evidence of the fact that only the big three wrote tragedies worthy of the name.

Another form of public entertainment are the Panhellenic, or 'All Greek', Games. The most prestigious are the Olympic Games, which are held every four years in the sanctuary of Zeus Olympios at Olympia, in the northwest Peloponnese. There are three other Panhellenic Games which attract spectators and competitors from all over the Greek world: the Isthmian, Nemean and Pythian. The first contest to be established was at Olympia in 776 BCE. This was a footrace over the distance of one stade, i.e. about 200m. Our word 'stadium' comes from 'stade'. Incidentally, 776 BCE is the first secure date in Greek history, being the year of the first Olympiad. These are held once every four years, as today. The Olympic Games will last into the Roman Era. The modern series was revived in 1896.

Such is the importance of these games that a sacred truce is proclaimed for their duration and all wars are suspended. (That is not the case with the modern series, the games being cancelled in 1916, 1940 and 1944.) The prize is a simple olive wreath, made of a branch from Zeus' sacred olive grove in Olympia. An Olympic victor earns enormous prestige, both for himself and for his city-state, and is treated like a conquering hero when he returns home, rather like the team that wins the Cup Final.

Athletes running.

110

War

What it's like to serve in the military

War is endemic in ancient Greece. Everybody's squabbling all the time, often for no better reason than that *polis* X has a long-standing grudge against *polis* Y, whose origin lies buried in the mists of time. Greece is divided by mountain ranges and that is one of the reasons why it never became united except as a result of conquest, first by the Macedonians and later by the Romans.

It's important to think of military service not as a burden. Your compatriots certainly don't. On the contrary, they think of it as a privilege; no less a privilege than attending the Assembly. If you follow their lead, you won't find it irksome at all. Or at any rate, you'll find it marginally less irksome. As a citizen, you will be liable to conscription from the age of eighteen to fifty-nine. Each of the ten tribes is called up on a yearly rotating basis. This means that you will always be serving with the same cadre of soldiers whom you will encounter in other contexts, which is very good for discipline and morale.

I don't know how much time you're going to have to spend on military training, outside of the periods when you're actually serving, but it will certainly be in your interests to keep fit. If you're a Spartan, you'll be constantly doing push-ups and lifting weights.

Saying goodbye to your family will be a very poignant experience, as it is in any society today. Bear in mind, moreover, that once you've bid them farewell, your loved ones won't hear any news about you until you return home, either alive or in cinerary urn.

Women, of course, don't serve in the military. If you're foolish enough to suggest that they should be allowed to do so, the Greeks will look at you as if you're completely off your rocker. They'd think you

Amphora depicting Achilles slaying the warrior queen Penthesilea.

were even battier if you suggest a woman could be a commander-in-chief. That said, the Greeks did conceive of a contingent of women fighters, the mythological Amazons, literally the 'Without-a-breasters', so named because they cut off their right breasts to facilitate their prowess as archers.

There's a strong socio-economic divide between service in the army and service in the navy. To serve in the army, you have to provide your own armour, and this is a costly investment, unless you happen to have inherited it from your father. Rowers only need an oar.

Hoplite fighting isn't about acts of derring-do. It's about standing lock-step in battle formation alongside your companions. You'll fight in what is called a phalanx, a rectangular formation several lines deep. Your shield is so big that it half-protects the soldier standing on your left, so if you advance or retreat other than in formation, you're going to put his life as well as your own in danger. You're armed with a spear, which you use for jabbing, rather than for throwing.

The average hoplite battle lasts less than an hour. That's because it's exhausting fighting in such conditions. The objective is not to annihilate the enemy but to cause him to retreat after suffering heavy losses. Once you've forced him to withdraw, you erect a trophy at the place where the course of the battle turned, using the spoils the enemy left behind. Our word 'trophy' comes from the Greek verb *trephein*, which means 'to turn'. You cremate your dead on the battlefield and bring their ashes back home. A Panhellenic law, subscribed to by all Greeks, requires the victorious army to permit the vanquished enemy to retrieve their dead from the battlefield. This law is almost never violated.

If you don't have any hoplite armour then you'll have to serve in the navy as a rower. Rowers are just as important as hoplites; perhaps even more so, since Athens' empire is maritime and her very survival depends on her navy. She has the largest fleet in the Greek world; about 250 triremes. A trireme is a ship with three banks of oars and a large sail. It's the greyhound of the seas. About 170 rowers serve on each trireme plus thirty other personnel, including some hoplites. This amounts to a total naval complement of 50,000, some of whom are metics. That, of course, is not including all those

Amphora depicting trireme.

who labour in the shipyards, though most of these are slaves.

Though you can be called upon to serve in the military up to the age of fifty-nine, the chances are that once you hit fifty, or perhaps less, you'll be required only to do garrison duty, protecting the walls that surround Athens and its port city, the Piraeus. A bit of a breeze compared to fighting.

Rowing for Athens

If it weren't for her rowers, Athens wouldn't have an empire. All her allies, that's to say, the cities she protects against Persian aggression, are situated on or beside the water. Their populations either inhabit the islands dotted around the Aegean Sea or live in coastal cities.

Rowing in the Athenian navy isn't for sissies. You have to be as tough as nails and disciplined with it. If you catch a crab, you might break all your ribs, not to say imperil the safety of your mates.

Athenian ships are called triremes. They're the most beautiful and swiftest ships ever built. They're extremely light and can virtually turn on a drachma. Well, that's a *slight* exaggeration. They can do a complete about-turn in less than two ships' length.

A trireme has three tiers on which the rowers sit. Each rower has a seat assigned to him with a leather cushion. Serving on the top tier requires the most skill and strength because the oars are highest out of the water. When the rowing master gives the order for the rowers to put their backs into it, they can reach a top speed of nine to ten knots.

A trireme is financed by a wealthy Athenian called a trierarch. Once appointed, the trierarch devotes as much money as he likes to maintain his trireme in shipshape condition, so to speak. There's a strong element of competition in making his ship look the best and be the fastest in the fleet. He can even captain it, if he chooses.

Most rowers live in the Piraeus. Once they've been summoned by a trumpet blast, they grab their oar from what is known as the Arsenal, belt down to the shipshed where their trireme is berthed and ease it down the ramp into the water. Then they scramble on board, take their assigned place on the bench, and on command start rowing like a bat out of Hades.

The rowing season lasts about five months, from May to September. The rest of the year rowers practise manoeuvres and do repairs. They have to know how to seal a leaking joint, stitch a ripped canvas, or replace a smashed beam. Triremes need constant upkeep and sometimes a fleet is away for months on end.

If you become a rower, you'll discover there's nothing more thrilling than ramming an enemy ship broadside, smashing into its hull with your bronze prow. It's terrifying for the enemy to see an Athenian trireme heading towards them at full speed. The howls and screams of the poor devils are truly blood-curdling. Sometimes a trireme slices the enemy ship in two. Another tactic is to sail close alongside an enemy ship and smash its oars like so many twigs before its commander can order his oarsmen to raise them out of the water. The ship will tilt over and become a sitting duck. Hoplites from your ship will then board it and lay into the defenseless rowers on the top tier, while those in the lower two tiers slowly drown as their ship takes on water.

One of the proudest moments for an Athenian rower had nothing to do with a naval battle. It happened eight years ago in the aftermath of the Mytilenean Revolt. Mytilene is one of Athens' most important allies, so the revolt was a serious threat to her security. After the Athenians had successfully besieged the city, they held a debate in the Assembly about what punishment to inflict on the prisoners. Some speakers urged clemency, others wholesale destruction. When the motion was put to the vote, a slender majority decided to execute all the men and enslave the women and children.

Once the Assembly ended, however, there was a sense of general unease. A lot of Athenians thought it was too harsh a punishment. In fact so many of them were unhappy with the decision that they immediately went to the Council and persuaded it to hold another Assembly the next day.

The politician who recommended wholesale massacre was called Cleon. He argued that this would send a stern message to any other city contemplating revolt. The most forceful advocate for leniency was Diodotus, who pointed out that if they executed all the male population of Mytilene, it would only make things worse in the future. That's because once the decision to revolt had been taken, all the citizens would join the resistance even if they had opposed it, since now they would have nothing to lose. The second debate was no less heated than the first, but this time the People voted by a narrow margin to execute only the ringleaders.

The problem was that a trireme with the order to execute the entire population had already been dispatched to Mytilene. A second trireme sailed off to countermand it. Mytileneans resident in Athens promised a handsome reward to the rowers of the second trireme if they arrived in time to save their compatriots.

It was a race against time. Unbelievably, the second ship arrived at the *exact* moment when the original decree was being read out. The first trireme had sailed super slow, its men being reluctant to carry out such a terrible command. If the second one had arrived even moments later, it would have been too late.

Diodotus was right. He wasn't arguing for mercy. He was arguing for commonsense.

Casualties and veterans

Casualties in hoplite warfare are perhaps as high as ten per cent. If you suffer injury, you'll receive rudimentary medical care. Amputations are a frequent occurrence, always with the danger that the stump will become infected. And of course, there are no anaesthetics or painkillers. In a naval battle the casualty rate depends on whether a ship sinks. If it does, there's a good chance most of the crew will drown. For some unfathomable reason, the Athenian state doesn't require its sailors to learn how to swim.

If you're lucky enough to return home victorious, don't expect to be fêted. All citizens serve in the military, so that's no big deal. A ceremony is held annually in the Ceramicus at the end of the fighting season to honour those who have died in the twelve months previously. The ashes of the dead are placed in ten large coffins for each of the ten tribes with an extra coffin for those whose bodies could not be identified.

If a veteran can prove to the satisfaction of the Council of 500 that he's unable to support himself owing to disability, he's entitled to a state pension. However, it's pretty miserly; one obol per day. An obol is one-sixth of a drachma, which is the daily wage of a hoplite.

The orphaned sons of fathers who die in battle are maintained at the state's expense. When they achieve adulthood, they participate in a graduation ceremony held during the Great Dionysia; the same festival at which plays are performed.

Fighting in the hoplite ranks

The most venerated Athenian hoplites are the ones who fought at the Battle of Marathon in 490. They'll all be dead by the time you arrive in 420 but their reputation will live on forever. The comic poet Aristophanes made them the chorus of one of his plays, called *Acharnians*. Many of the hoplites who fought at Marathon came from the deme of Acharnae, in the far north of Attica. Aristophanes portrayed them as crusty old sods, opposed to making peace with the Spartans, but his portrait was an affectionate one all the same. If the Marathon men had lost the battle, the Persians would have destroyed Athens.

Marathon lies on the northeast coast of Attica, opposite the long island of Euboea, twenty-six miles from Athens. The Persian king Darius had sent an expedition to exact revenge on both Athens and Eretria, a *polis* on the west coast of Euboea, for assisting the Ionian Greeks who inhabit the modern-day Turkish coast in a doomed revolt.

The Athenians and Eretrians had attacked the city of Sardis and destroyed the great temple of Artemis. They had failed to take the city, however, and sailed back home, abandoning the Ionians to their fate.

Having burned Eretria to the ground, the Persians crossed the straits between Euboea and Attica and landed in the Bay of Marathon. It was now the Athenians' turn to face the music. Panic took hold of them. The People couldn't agree whether to defend Athens or march to Marathon. After a heated debate they decided to march to Marathon.

They also dispatched their fastest long-distance runner, a man called Philippides, to Sparta – 150 miles away – to seek military assistance. The Spartans expressed their deepest sympathy, but excused themselves on the grounds that they were celebrating a religious festival in honour of Apollo and wouldn't be able to lend assistance till it was over. You can always rely on the Spartans to let you down.

When Philippides arrived at Marathon, everyone was despondent at first. It wasn't all bad news, however. It turned out that he had met Pan on his way back. The goat god had promised to fight for the Athenians, on condition that they rewarded him with a public cult.

There was a lot of disagreement among the board of generals about what course of action to take. Back then it was the policy that a different general should be commander-in-chief each day. Eventually a general called Miltiades opted to join battle. As per normal, a seer performed a sacrifice, a hymn was sung, and Miltiades gave the order to charge. Your compatriots let out a blood-curdling cry and ran full-tilt towards the Persians, carefully maintaining strict battle-order; no easy feat. There's an event at the Olympic Games over approximately the same distance called the 'hoplite-run', in which contestants race against each other clad in war gear, so the lads were fully up for the challenge. Just before they came within striking distance of the Persians, they lowered their spears and crashed into them like a ton of bricks.

A hoplite battle is about as intense an experience as you can imagine. You can't see much other than what lies directly ahead because you have only two narrow eye slits in your helmet. It's impossible to hear orders once you come to close combat, due to the din of battle, added to which your heart is pounding in your chest. You just have to go on instinct most of the time, trying to stay close to the man on your right because his shield overlaps and protects you. In most hoplite battles, the winner is content merely to take possession of the field and erect a trophy decorated with enemy spoils. Then everyone goes back home. But the Athenians were fighting for their survival.

The Persians had never seen armed soldiers charging full-tilt at them before. Many stayed rooted to the spot. Some turned tail and fled, flinging their shields away. They 'panicked', in other words, by which I mean that Pan did his stuff, just as he'd promised, as the god of panic. Once the Athenians came to close quarters, they jabbed with their spears, and when their spears became useless, they threw them down and used their swords.

The battle lasted less than an hour. Eventually the Persians fled to their ships and tried to sail off. It was very difficult for them to navigate in the shallow bay, however, and the Athenians were able to inflict more casualties as they scrambled to make their getaway.

That wasn't the end of the matter. Miltiades ordered the victors to march or rather trot back to defend the city against attack. Despite being exhausted, nobody complained. Spirits couldn't have been higher.

When they arrived at Phaleron Bay five miles south of Athens, the Persians were preparing to disembark. Observing the Athenians lining up on the beach, however, they thought better of it and sailed off. And that is how Pan came to acquire his cult in a cave on the north side of the Acropolis.

Losses on the Athenian side were just 192. The Persian dead amounted to 6,500. The People voted to give heroic honours to the 192 and perform a state sacrifice in their honour every year. They buried their ashes on the battlefield instead of bringing them back to

Athens, which was the usual practice. You'll see the mound which contains their remains. It marks the spot where the battle turned in Athens' favour. It's still there to this day.

The only sad part of the story is what happened to Philippides. Following the victory, he volunteered to run back to Athens with the news, but after delivering it he collapsed on the spot and died. He'd covered the distance from Athens to Sparta in record time and had hardly rested before belting off to Athens, sprinting those now famous twenty-six miles.

There was something uncanny about the battle. The Athenians didn't deserve to win, not by any normal calculation, but once they started charging they proved unstoppable. If they'd lost, democracy would have been dead in the water.

Law and Order

How Athens is policed

There's no police force as such, so it's up to the neighbourhood watch or its equivalent to take note of and act upon any crime. Since Athens is what anthropologists call a face-to-face society, that's to say, one where a large number of people recognise one another, a burglar would have considerable difficulty escaping detection. Obviously, too, it's in everyone's interests to make sure that criminals are punished; a fact that contributes to vigilance on the part of the community. For the same reason, wrongdoing is often 'settled' in the community in one way or another, with the result that many criminals are never charged for their crimes. Athens, in other words, is self-policed.

Crime and criminality

One of the most fascinating questions to ask about the ancient world in general, and also one that is virtually impossible to answer, is 'What is the crime rate?' We have no statistics to help us understand the incidence of any specific crime or of crime in general. Statistics haven't been invented and there's little consciousness of a social trend.

What we can say without fear of contradiction is that Sparta is more law-abiding than Athens, with the proviso that Spartan youths are free, and to some degree even encouraged, to murder helots. Though a large number of Athenian law court speeches have survived, most deal with what we would call white-collar crime, such as falsely claiming an inheritance. Rarely do we hear of crimes of violence. We shouldn't for that reason assume they don't occur, of course. As I mentioned a moment ago, most crimes against persons or property are probably settled in other ways.

The really big question is whether Classical Athens in particular and ancient Greece in general are more law-abiding than modern societies, and that's a question we can't begin to answer. As a result, I can't give you much advice on this topic. I hope you'll feel safer than you would in a modern city. You'll be hearing in a moment from an Athenian who was recently beaten up in the Agora.

Going to trial

Just as there is no police force, so, too, there is no public prosecutor. Responsibility for bringing an action against a wrongdoer therefore lies with the victim. If it's a crime against the state, however, 'anyone who wishes' is permitted to bring the action. That's how Socrates will be brought to trial: three private individuals who have nothing to do with him will charge him with crimes which they allege were injurious to the state. The complainant appeals to one of the archons. If the archon determines that the charge has merit, he will summon the defendant and assign a day for the trial proceedings to take place.

The accused is prosecuted in court before a jury of his peers, just like in our system. Unless caught red-handed, he will remain at liberty until the day of his trial, irrespective of the severity of the charge. Many accused, fearing a guilty verdict, take this opportunity to flee abroad rather than face justice. Unless it is a crime against the state, no effort will be made to apprehend them and bring them to trial. 'Good riddance' is the general attitude.

Juries are invariably large, some with as many as 601 jurors. The plaintiff speaks first, followed without interval by the defendant. Both have an equal amount of time to present their case. There are no witnesses, though statements taken in advance can be read out in court. If a slave has been required to give testimony, this will have happened under torture. That's because torture is believed to be 'the best test of truth', in the words of a fourth-century speechwriter called Isaeus. There's a judge who conducts the trial, but his role is merely to supervise the proceedings and keep order. Since trials take place in the open, speakers regularly have to deal with heckling from outside the court, turning the trial into a form of spectator sport. After plaintiff and defendant have both spoken, the jurors immediately retire to vote in secret. There's no time set aside for deliberation.

Once the votes have been counted, the jurors return to court and their verdict is read out. If a majority of merely one has found the defendant guilty, both the defendant and the plaintiff will recommend a penalty, except in cases where a penalty is prescribed by law. For instance, burglary, larceny, the kidnapping of slaves, treason and impiety all carry an automatic penalty of death. The most common penalty is either a fine, the loss of civic rights or exile. Sentencing a person found guilty to a term of imprisonment is not an option because the state does not have the resources to provide for prisoners at public expense. Only those who represent a flight risk, like Socrates, who will be condemned to death, are incarcerated, and then only in the brief interval between conviction and execution.

If the plaintiff fails to secure one-fifth of the votes of the jury, he will be fined 1,000 drachmas as punishment for malicious prosecution. Neither side can launch an appeal on any grounds whatsoever. The whole process generally lasts at most half a day.

Travel

Ways of travel

Many Greeks walk long distances on a regular basis, whether for recreation or for work. At the beginning of Plato's *Republic* Socrates has walked five miles from Athens to the Piraeus to witness a festival and he would have returned to Athens the same day, had he not been spotted by a friend, who urged him to come back to his house. A minority of Greeks travel by cart. In the countryside, it's a pretty common sight to see men and women riding on an ass or a donkey. Horses are pretty useless over

Horseman.

any distance due to the roughness of the terrain. For the same reason, chariots are unsuitable as a method of transport. The mountainous nature of the landscape is partly why the system of independent city-states has grown up, since it's generally very difficult to get from one *polis* to another.

Paved roads extend for only short distances and they primarily serve the purpose of enabling festival processions to make stately progress from their point of departure towards the sanctuary of the deity being celebrated. Their purpose is, therefore, ceremonial rather than utilitarian. Mostly what you'll encounter are dirt tracks.

If you want to get anywhere really quickly, I suggest you run. The chances are that your feet are calloused and have been since you were a child, so you'll hardly be conscious of the rocks and the brambles you'll encounter along the way. Of course, that's only an option if you're a man. A woman can hardly hitch up her dress and expose her knees, except under dire emergency.

Bear in mind there will be constant danger of attack from footpads and wild animals. The altercation that takes place between Oedipus and Laius on the road from Delphi to Thebes, which leads to the death of Laius, is entirely true to life in that, once you're out on the open road, you may easily find yourself in a life-threatening situation.

Ox-drawn carts are the best way of transporting heavy loads, but note that an ox, even when it's belting along at top speed, manages only about two miles per hour.

Greece has virtually no navigable rivers and none that bind communities together. To compensate for that deficiency, there's an extensive nexus of connections between communities that have access to the sea. Overseas trade is a significant part of the economy of many city-states. Pirates, however, are a perennial hazard, so much so that piracy is almost an accepted way of life. It was because of the fear of piracy that Athens was founded five miles from the coast. And then there are the squalls that Poseidon whips up.

Where to stay when travelling

In urban areas, ports especially, you'll find plenty of facilities that pose as hotels. Unfortunately, you'll have to cope with the fact that many of them are home to bedbugs and other kinds of creepy crawlies, including rats. In the countryside, hotels simply don't exist. This deficiency is somewhat alleviated by the importance that the Greeks place on hospitality. Among aristocrats, hospitality is formalised into an institution known as guest-friendship or *xenia*. In accordance with the rules of *xenia*, an aristocrat is permitted to arrive unannounced at the home of a fellow-aristocrat who is his guest-friend and can expect to be hosted for an indefinite period of time. This arrangement comes under the protection of no less a deity than Zeus Xenios, and it's a prominent feature of the society that Homer depicts in the *Odyssey*. It enables aristocrats not only to travel safely abroad, but also to build enduring links with fellow-aristocrats in foreign communities. Though *xenia* is primarily an aristocratic institution, commoners, too, can develop ties outside their communities, and this enables them to travel more modest distances.

A Final Word of Advice

There's no doubt that adjusting to ancient Greece is going to be something of a challenge. Life, as you will have gathered, is lived without amenities, without labour-saving devices, and without the many distractions that enable us in the twenty-first century to escape the harshness of reality. All basic tasks, like washing clothes and making bread, have to be done by hand. You or your slaves will spend many hours each day performing routine activities. You rise at dawn and often go to sleep at dusk.

You cannot refrigerate and ice isn't available, so your food will quickly go off. Food shortages are common since harvests are unpredictable, which means you're probably going to have to tighten your belt at times. Just the act of keeping alive is going to be so much more difficult.

You may find yourself living with a number of your relatives in a single room. Your slaves will know all your business since it's virtually impossible to keep any secrets from them.

You'll be almost wholly dependent on your friends for entertainment, other than on the rare times in the year when dramatic performances are taking place. I recommend that you put a very high premium on conversation. Though you are probably literate to some degree, I doubt you'll have much money to spend on scrolls, the ancient equivalent of books.

You're going to be living much closer to the edge in all kinds of ways. Your vulnerability to accident, disease, famine, fire and war is reflected in the fickleness, jealousy and vengefulness of your gods.

I strongly recommend that you put something away for a rainy day, though I doubt you will take my advice, not least because you probably won't have the luxury of looking to the future. Only the wealthy have money and resources to spare.

If you become sick or incapacitated as a result of injury or old age, don't expect the state, i.e. your fellow citizens, to step in. The state doesn't see it as its duty to care for its citizens in their time of need, except in the case of a few disabled. This means that if you don't have any family member or friend to lean on, it'll be very difficult for you to ride out the many crises that will inevitably occur during your lifetime. From a very early age you will be stalked by death, both by the deaths of those close to you and by death-threatening occurrences.

The rule is that dog eats dog; literally. That reminds me, always carry a few stones to ward off any animal that approaches you. Most of the dogs you'll see outdoors will be starving. They'd just as soon take a bite out of your leg as lick your hand.

I hope I haven't put you off too much. There are also many compensations to justify your moving to Classical Athens. Your *oikos* will be a much closer-knit structure than families are generally today. You'll feel a stronger degree of kinship to a much larger community than most people do today. Your *polis* will be more homogeneous and unified than virtually any modern society. I don't mean ethnically homogeneous, though that is a fact to take into account. I mean that all the members of the *polis*, slaves included, are facing certain inescapable existential imperatives. Of these, the principal imperative is life's unpredictability. In other words, everyone is very much in the same boat.

You'll be relieved to know that feelings of guilt won't trouble you much, though shame will to a much greater degree than it does in our society. In fact it's shame, not guilt, that will motivate you to do the right thing, like fighting valiantly when you would rather slink away.

Unless you happen to be standing beside an odiferous pile of dung, you'll find the air is pure to a degree that you may never have experienced before. From the Acropolis on a good day you will be able to see all the way to Acrocorinth in the Peloponnese, some 60 miles distant. And at night the stars will be more plentiful and brighter than they are almost anywhere in the developed world today. And there won't be any chemicals in your food.

Racism is largely unknown. It's true that the Greeks call non-Greeks, including Persians, barbarians, but it seems that that pejorative term derives chiefly from the incomprehensibility of non-Greek speech, which to a Greek ear sounds like 'ba-ba-ba'. The term became common during the period of the Graeco-Persian Wars, when the Persians presented a lethal threat to the Greeks. After the war ended, the prejudice largely dissipated. You're unlikely to encounter any colour prejudice. You may even discover that the Greeks are darker-skinned than you will be expecting.

Greek women are generally subject to male authority, but don't assume that if you return to ancient Greece as a woman you will automatically be complaining about your lot in life, even if you're stuck at home. You might see certain advantages in being looked after, even at the cost of your personal liberty. There are so many hazards and threats out there. If you're adventurous and enterprising, you might consider becoming a *hetaira*. You'd certainly be mixing with some interesting people and your views would be taken seriously.

Don't take your twenty-first century sensibility with you. You're not going to encounter anyone debating the ethics of slavery or advocating women's liberation. You'll have to accept that slavery is an unalterable fact of life. Aristotle in *Politics* writes, 'It's not only necessary but also expedient that some should rule and others be ruled, and from the moment of their birth some are marked out to be subjected, others to subject.'

You're going to have to be sparing of your compassion. You're bound to encounter many situations where the instinct to do good has to give way to the simple need for survival. If food runs short, for instance, you will have to favour the breadwinners over those who are non-productive. Some elderly people may starve as a result of what anthropologists call benign neglect. There's nothing to be done about it; that's life. You may also have to make some very hard decisions about which children to rear, which to favour, and even which to feed; the kind of decisions that would be deeply offensive to a twenty-first century sensibility. You'll also see some very distressing sights. Many people are disabled and disfigured. The majority of Athenians are very poor by our standards, though only a tiny fraction of them are actually impoverished, perhaps as little as one per cent. About the same percentage are really wealthy.

Your sense of hearing will be much more acute. You'll be able to pick up sounds from a far greater distance. Your sense of smell will be more intense as well. That's because you'll be more reliant on these senses for your safety than you are today. In the absence of spreadsheets, filing cabinets, and the like, your memory will be vastly superior. You'll be able to remember long passages of literature, deliver lengthy speeches, and reel off information effortlessly. Everything will be safely stored in that complex computer we call the brain. Once you age, of course, it's a different matter, but at least until the age of thirty, perhaps older, your sensory awareness will be much sharper.

Then there are all the dubious technological advances that you'll be spared. You won't have to bother with e-mail and your children won't be texting every hour of the day and night. You'll be able to focus on the important things of life without being constantly interrupted and distracted.

This is obvious but it's worth stating all the same. There isn't any pollution, there are no ugly pylons or telephone poles crisscrossing the landscape, no rumble of a motorway even in the depths of the countryside, no oil slicks, and no mountains of industrial waste. Natural hazards occur with considerable frequency, of course, but you won't be complaining of stress. Though mental illness almost certainly exists, it's far less frequent than in the modern world. The remedy for many of life's problems in antiquity is simply to get on with life.

And if you have an ounce of sensibility, which you surely do, the beauty of the natural world, uncontaminated by the human species, will knock your non-existent socks off.

Greeks poets are always banging on about the misery of human existence and wishing they were dead. 'Not to be born in the first place is best for men on earth, or if born to pass through the gates of Hades as quickly as possible,' writes gloomy old Sophocles. Likewise, Herodotus reports that when a mother prayed to the goddess Hera to bestow the greatest good on her two sons, they both fell asleep in the night and died a painless death. But is that the majority view? I seriously doubt it. Most Greeks, I suspect, relish life to the full, and it is for that reason above all that I would love to return to ancient Greece and why I recommend you do too.

The injunction to 'seize the day' is familiar to us through the Latin phrase *carpe diem*, but the Romans were only copying the Greeks, as in so much else. It's the Greeks who coined the concept. This injunction, coupled with the brevity and precariousness of existence, adds greatly to the intensity which they experience in being alive.

Like the late lamented Robin Williams in *Dead Poets' Society*, they whisper those words in my ears every day of my life.

Testimonials

This section of the book features a number of interviews with Greeks from different walks of life and different places. It is hoped that these will help you to see the world from their perspective and further prepare you for what to expect.

Hippocleia, an aristocratic Athenian girl

'I've been lucky so far. None of my brothers or sisters has died and my parents are extremely rich and aristocratic. I'm also attractive. My father has had four offers of marriage for me already and I'm only twelve! I thank the gods for all the blessings they've given me.

'My family are Eteoboutads. The Eteoboutads are the most noble Athenian *genos* of all. The only *genos* that comes close is the Alcmaeonid. I wouldn't want to be an Alcmaeonid, though. Alcmaeonids are cursed. A long time ago they committed an act of sacrilege so terrible that the gods could never forgive them. An act of sacrilege is when you offend the gods big time. Their ancestors murdered some suppliants when they were clasping the knees of the goddess Athena on the Acropolis. Suppliants are under divine protection. It's one of the gravest sins to kill people when they're supplicating a deity.

'Daddy can't stand the Alcmaeonids. There's a young Alcmaeonid called Alcibiades, whom he really hates. Alcibiades makes all the girls and boys swoon. He's terribly good-looking and even richer than Daddy. He owns lots of racehorses and he's won prizes in the chariot races at the Olympic Games. Daddy says Alcibiades only thinks about himself but I'd love to be his wife. Alcmaeonids never marry Eteoboutads, however, so there's no chance of that. Besides, Alcibiades is already married to an ugly old duck called Hipparete, though there's a rumour going around that he's planning to divorce her.

'Daddy says that it was an Alcmaeonid called Pericles who got us into the terrible war with the Spartans. Daddy actually likes Spartans and has lots of Spartan friends, so he hates the war. He doesn't like the democracy either, though I'm supposed not to tell anyone that. He thinks most people are ignorant and stupid and shouldn't have the power they have. He says the war against the Spartans is stupid as well and that no good will come of it.

'Aristocratic girls like myself are very important in Athens, as the story of Athens' first king Erechtheus proves. Erechtheus' mummy was Athena. She brought him up in her temple on the Acropolis, where the big snake lives. When Erechtheus was an adult, he became king and had to fight a battle against the people of Eleusis, who lived west of what now is the land called Attica. He went to Delphi to ask Apollo how he could win. Apollo replied that the only way he could win was if he sacrificed one of his daughters. Imagine that!

'Erechtheus didn't know which one to sacrifice because he had three daughters and he loved them all equally. However, the one called Chthonia – her name means 'Earthy' – said, "Daddy, I'll sacrifice myself for the good of Athens." She was very brave, you see. Her daddy agreed because he had to win the war and punish the people of Eleusis. But then Chthonia's two sisters told him they didn't want her to die alone, because they were all very close and could never bear to be parted, so he ended up sacrificing all three. It's a very sad story, and Erechtheus died of a broken heart and became the snake that lives on the Acropolis.

'Mummy says it all turned out for the best in the end, however, because it was thanks to Erechtheus' daughters that Athens won the war against Eleusis. I'd sacrifice myself for Athens, if Daddy asked me to, though I hope he won't. Eteoboutads are noble, you see, and it's right that people look up to us and think we're special. Even so, I don't think my baby sister Calliope would volunteer to die with me. She's a selfish little pig and I hope she gets bitten by a rat.

'Only Eteoboutads can become priests of Poseidon Erechtheus. Poseidon made a jet of water spring up on the Acropolis in the hope that we'd name the city Poseidonia in his honour, instead of Athens. But the judge, whose name was Cecrops, was more impressed by Athena's gift of an olive tree. That's why our city is called Athens. That's also why there are so many olive trees in Attica and why Daddy is so rich because he owns a huge olive grove. Poseidon couldn't un-gift his gift, however,

Olive grove.

gods can never do that, so that's why we have the most powerful navy in the world, all because of the jet of water. It's clear the gods love us heaps and heaps.

'When I was seven, Mummy and Daddy took me to Brauron, a seaside deme on the east coast of Attica. Brauron has a big sanctuary of Artemis, the goddess who protects wild animals. Artemis is a virgin. She doesn't want anything to do with men. Girls have to be very careful not to make her angry. If she finds out you're going to get married and you don't bring her a present, she'll punish you. If you're aristocratic like me, your parents take you to her sanctuary and leave you there for a few days. The priestess of Artemis gives you a yellow dress and teaches you a game called "how to play the bear." It's a lot of fun. You have to pretend you're a bear with claws and then you get tamed and at the end of your stay at Brauron your Mummy and Daddy take you home and they're very happy because you've made Artemis happy and now she won't do anything nasty to you like make you die when you're giving birth. One or two girls I've known who were bears did die giving birth, but Mummy says that was because they didn't give all their toys to Artemis when they started having their periods. I'll certainly give Artemis all my toys when I start having periods. I don't want to take any risks!

'Daddy says I'm going to be *kanêphoros*, a basket bearer, for Athena at the Panathenaea festival next year. That's if I'm not married by then!'

Phainarete, a widow

'Timon, my husband died last year in a tragic accident. He owned a shield factory and was very wealthy. The roof of his factory collapsed because of the weight of the shields stored up in the rafters. He wasn't killed outright. It would have been better if he had. Two of his workers who survived the accident carried him back home. His chest was crushed and he could hardly breathe. He was in agony for days till he finally heaved his last.

'Timon was a good husband to me. He worked hard, was an upstanding citizen, and provided well for his family. Four of our nine children survived infancy. Milo, the eldest, is now twelve. Archippe, the youngest, is only two. We owned four slaves: one to look after our children, another to do the shopping and the cooking, and two to work in the fields.

'My husband hardly ever fooled around with them. That's pretty rare these days. I'd certainly have known it if he had. You can always tell because favoured slaves become uppity. Of course, what he did outside the home is another matter altogether. But what happens outside the home stays outside the home is the best motto. He came home to bed every night, even if he was a bit the worse for wear at times.

'When he died it was terrible for me, because I found out that he owed a lot of money to his bronze-supplier. He hadn't been able to pay his debt because he was waiting to be reimbursed for a consignment of shields he'd just sold. When the man who'd purchased the shields found out that I was a widow, he refused to settle his account. He knew I couldn't take any legal action because I was the weakest of the weak and there wasn't anyone I could appeal to. My parents had both died several years ago and I didn't have any brothers or uncles to protect me.

'I had to give the bronze-supplier almost all of Timon's savings. The house had to be sold and I moved in with my aunt Nikagora. Nikagora is also a widow. Between us we have eight children to raise. At least Timon's father had the decency to return my dowry. Nikagora survives by making wicker baskets and dyeing ribbons to make sashes for tombs and temples.

'I only hope I live long enough to see all my children married. I certainly can't afford to give all my girls dowries. I'll be thirty on my next birthday, so I'm getting on. I've never got my full strength back from my last pregnancy. The baby was stillborn and I got a bad infection. It nearly carried me off.

'I know I sound like a hard-luck case, but I'm grateful to the gods for all they've given me. I always remember that bit in Homer's *Iliad* about the two jars of Zeus. One contains good fortune and the other bad, and if you're lucky Zeus gives you good fortune mixed with bad. If you're not, he only gives you bad fortune. I'm one of the lucky ones because I've had good fortune mixed with bad. I had a happy childhood, a happy marriage, and I've got four healthy children. Of course, you never know what's lying around the corner, but if you sacrifice and pray to the gods, they'll see you'll be all right in the end.'

Diogenes, a politician

'Even as a young boy I was fascinated by public speaking. I used to hover outside the Pnyx, where meetings of the Assembly take place, straining to hear the politicians argue with one another. Public speaking requires expertise, clear-headedness, self-confidence, charisma, a flair for the dramatic, a command of language, and, finally, the ability to think on your feet, both literally as well as figuratively. I'm fortunate to be blessed with all those qualities in spades, even though I say so myself.

'I had the great good fortune to study under the esteemed sophist Gorgias of Leontini, who taught in Athens when I was a young man. He had an international reputation, and deservedly so. He was particularly famous for assigning his students the most difficult rhetorical exercises imaginable. The one that I remember to this day was having to prove that Helen, a flagrant adulteress who betrayed her husband, Menelaus, by running off with Paris, was the most chaste woman who has ever lived. Gorgias taught us all the tricks of the trade, so that by the time he'd finished with us, we could argue the hind legs off a donkey. And that, whether you like to admit it or not, is essential in my line of business.

'In short, I owe my not inconsiderable success as a public speaker to Gorgias. Nobody can succeed in the Assembly if he hasn't got a sound foundation in rhetoric. Public speaking is all about being able to sway, and if necessary, seduce the crowd. Bear in mind that there are about 6,000 citizens present. Most of them are pretty ignorant so you have to work overtime to woo them. The crowd likes nothing better than a no-holds-barred fight between two leading politicians, and at the end of it many of them side with the one who has produced the cleverer argument, irrespective of whether it's right or not. That's our democracy for you and long may it flourish!

'It also helped my career – I'll readily admit it – that I come from a wealthy family. As you know, one of the best ways to get recognition in Athens is by financing a dramatic chorus or by paying for a trireme, and you can only do that if you're wealthy. I was wealthy enough to do both. That got me a lot of attention, and that means that the People listen to me whenever I have anything to say on any topic under discussion, which is pretty well all the time.

'As you can imagine, it takes a lot of courage to stand up before a large crowd. The first time I got up, I was trembling all over. It was a blisteringly cold day in the dead of winter and my voice got carried away by the wind. I remember people a few rows back shouting out, "Speak up, laddie! We can't hear you!" When I started stammering, they began mocking me. It was the most humiliating moment in my entire life. It was all I could do to prevent myself from bursting into tears there and then.

'That evening I went and told Gorgias what had happened. I was still snivelling, I don't mind admitting. Gorgias ordered me to get a grip of myself. He said I had to ignore the faces before me and focus on a spot in the distance. It was the best advice I've ever received. When I got the chairman's eye at the next meeting of the Assembly, it was a very different matter altogether. I ignored all the hecklers and kept my calm. I'm now highly respected. I even crossed swords, figuratively speaking, with Pericles, the year before he died.

'Pericles was my hero. He was our leading politician for nearly twenty years. What I admired most about him was the fact that he always managed to rise above the fray. Even under fire, he remained as cool as a clove of garlic. His enemies called him "the Olympian" because of his haughty demeanour. You think he tried to modify his behaviour in consequence? Far from it. He didn't give a damn whether the People were on his side or not. He was never afraid to speak his mind. He once said to them, "You're completely spineless. You seem incapable of sticking by the policies you've voted on. I'm the only one around here with any backbone." No one has ever been more indifferent to public opinion; and the People loved him for it.

'Like all politicians, Pericles made his mistakes, getting us embroiled in the war for starters. He was the one who said we shouldn't make any concessions to the Spartans. That's because he had total confidence in our fleet, which he said was the mightiest on the face of the earth. Well, he was right on that score. But then along came the plague and poor old Pericles became one of its victims; a victim, so to speak, of his own rhetoric. There's irony for you. I bet one or two of the gods enjoyed a chuckle over that. Hubris always comes before a fall.

'Even to this day it still helps to be an aristocrat when you address the Assembly because then you can round up a team of supporters. However, men with no social standing whatsoever are increasingly shooting their mouths off and rabble-rousing. They're a thoroughly bad lot, if you ask me. The worst of the bunch is Cleon. Cleon is a smelly tanner's son, if you can believe it. I have to give the devil his due, however. He knows how to stir up the People good and proper. He doesn't have any principles and he couldn't give a fig for Athens. One time he accused Nicias, our top general, of being weak. He said if he were general he could capture the Spartans who were giving us the run around on a tiny island called Sphacteria at the tip of the Peloponnese.

'When Nicias offered to resign his generalship in his favour, Cleon tried to wriggle out of it but the People wouldn't have it. I remember thinking at the time, well, one of two good things will come out of this: either we'll be shot of Cleon for good or he'll do what he promises and capture the Spartans. It's a win-win situation, in other words. To everyone's amazement Cleon followed through on his boast and captured the Spartans within days of landing on the island.

'Cleon represents the new breed of politicians who are only in it for themselves. I'm sorry to say that chaps like myself, who put the good of the state first, are a dying breed. I've always tried to promote what I think is in Athens' best interests, even when it's made me unpopular.

'Politicians don't receive any pay for their services. I sometimes think it would be better if they did because they're always being accused of accepting bribes. Well, corruption always lies at the core of politics. Even Pericles couldn't escape the charge. When King Archidamus made a point of not destroying Pericles' country estate at the beginning of the war, the People accused him of being in cahoots with the Spartans. He only managed to quell the rumour by donating his estate to the People. Say what you like about his policies, Pericles was a solid gent, the like of whom no longer exists today.

'I'm always banging on about the proud tradition of selfless patriotism that we have inherited, but most people don't give a toss. They're much more likely to follow the lead of blowhards like Cleon than they are of principled men like myself. Patriotism has gone down the tubes.'

Autocrates, a victim of crime

'Athens is a dangerous place, there's no getting away from it. Though the population is largely law-abiding, if you *do* find yourself the victim of a crime, you're entirely on your own. That's the first thing you need to know. It's true that there are Scythian archers to keep order at public meetings, but they won't come to your aid if, say, you're mugged, as I was when walking home late one night through the Agora.

'I was just passing the Temple of Hephaestus when two blokes came out of nowhere and set upon me. They knocked me to the ground, punched me in the face, and kicked me in the groin. By the time they ran off, I was badly bruised in several places and my new woollen cloak was torn and covered in blood. My leg was broken, so all I could do was hobble home as best I could, painfully dragging it behind me. I now walk with a permanent limp because I couldn't afford to have it set by a physician. I live from hand to mouth, like lots of Athenians. To make matters worse, the coins I was carrying in my mouth for safe keeping had fallen out during the attack and got scattered in the dust. I couldn't find them anywhere. All my worldly savings gone in one fell swoop.

'Though it was a moonless night, I recognised the faces of my two assailants. They were a father and son. I knew them from when I was on garrison duty at a border fort last year. They were an ugly pair, to put it mildly. We'd had an altercation over whose turn it was to keep watch.

The son got so irate that he'd emptied the contents of his chamber pot over the head of my slave. I reported them to their commanding officer next morning and he severely reprimanded them.

'They'd obviously been stalking me and saw a good chance to get their revenge. It was a thoroughly cowardly act. If they'd attacked me where I lived – I live in the deme of Alopeke, south of Athens – my neighbours would have come to my rescue.

'No one saw them beating me up so it was just their word against mine. The morning after the incident, even though I was in terrible pain, I hobbled round to the magistrate, showed him my broken leg, and lodged a complaint, accusing my assailants of causing grievous bodily harm. He summoned them to an arraignment a month or so later. They pleaded not guilty and the magistrate set a date for the trial. I knew others who had been assaulted by them in the past, so I began collecting depositions in order to demonstrate their persistent and habitual viciousness.

'Thanks to these depositions, I was able to convince the jury – 201 in all – that the defendants were dyed-in-the-wool criminals. It helped that I'd found out that the father had largely absented himself from the Council of 500 during his year as a councillor, a duty that every loyal citizen may be called upon to perform. I've never been a councillor myself, but I'm always hoping I'll get picked and if I do I'll fulfill my obligation punctiliously.

'I informed the jury that I'd never appeared in a court of law, either as a plaintiff or as a defendant. So many Athenians these days are litigious. Some even make a career out of bringing false charges in the hope of winning large settlements. I'm just an honest, hard-working citizen. My wife died giving birth a year ago and I've got two little ones to bring up. I attend the Assembly regularly, participate in all our great state festivals, and do my best to set an example of civic consciousness.

'After I'd said my piece, the father, Conon, got up. He's well-to-do, so he'd hired a professional speechwriter. He hadn't bothered to learn the speech, however, and stumbled as he read it. Employing a speechwriter rarely does much good in my view. The jury sees right through you. They knew he was delivering a clever speech written by a professional hack, whereas I was talking from the heart.

'When Conon was ordered to stop in mid-sentence as he'd run out of time, the jury rose to cast their ballots. There was no discussion, as you know. I'm happy to report that I won by 131 votes to 70. The judge instructed both Conon and myself to propose a punishment. Conon suggested a derisory fine of 50 drachmas, whereas I suggested 400. The jury voted again and this time the count was 152 to 49 in my favour.

'I hope that will teach them both a lesson they won't forget. It's a sign of the times that a father should be encouraging his son to break the law and do injury to an honest, hard-working and loyal citizen. Morals have been steadily declining. My neighbour got struck by his son last week. Imagine that! A son striking his own father! That certainly wouldn't happen in Sparta. Spartans have far more respect for their parents. I know it's not very patriotic of me to say this, but sometimes I wish I were living in Sparta. Everyone there practises obedience to the law. It's a very different story in Athens.'

Euthyphro, an aspiring philosopher

'I've always been interested in the really big questions, such as, "What's the basic stuff that everything is made of?" Thales was the first philosopher who tried to find the answer. Miletus, his home town, is on the west coast of Ionia. That's where philosophy was born.

'Thales lived three or four generations ago. It seems that no one had ever asked that question before. Or at least not without giving the credit for everything that exists to the gods. He concluded that the source of all things is water, which makes sense when you think about it. I mean, nothing can exist without water. Humans drink, animals drink, flowers drink. Thales was an amazing scientist as well. He predicted an eclipse of the sun.

'His pupil was Anaximander. Anaximander pointed out that one thing alone can't be the source of everything. For instance, if water is the source, where does fire come from? He came up with the idea of something called the *apeiron,* the limitless or unbounded, being the source of everything. There was a third Milesian philosopher called Anaximenes, who proposed that air is the source of all things. That makes perfect sense too. After all, air is all around us and all living things need it to exist.

'Don't worry. I'm not going to give you a crash course in philosophy. I'll just mention two other big names, whom I particularly revere. Heraclitus, who came from Ephesus, another city in Ionia, declared that nothing is permanent and that everything is in flux. "Everything flows," he said. Just those two words. He made his point by saying that no one can enter the same river twice since the water in the river is always changing. Parmenides, who came from Elea, a town in southern Italy, held the opposite view. He said that nothing can be created out of nothing and that what has been created is indestructible.

'I used to converse endlessly about all this with my friends. Sadly, that's not what philosophers are interested in these days. The natural world, by which I mean existence itself, isn't their main concern. That's because a generation or so ago along came the sophists, who began saying that those kinds of questions don't get you anywhere in life and are a total waste of time. The sophists maintain that we don't know anything for certain, so we might as well throw in the towel because the only thing that really matters – this, it turns out, is the one thing they *do* know for certain – is how to achieve success and the only way to do that is by learning how to win an argument. Sophists don't believe in anything outside the human frame of reference.

'The most famous sophist was Protagoras of Abdera. Abdera is a city in Thrace, up in the north. Protagoras was always hopping about from one place to another, earning huge fees for his lectures. Someone once asked him if the gods exist. He said no one could possibly know the answer, for two reasons: first, because the question was too complex, and second, because life is too short. He also said, "Man is the measure of all things. Of the being of things that are, and the non-being of things that are not." I can't honestly say I know what non-being is. When I asked Protagoras' compatriot, a philosopher called Democritus, if he knew what non-being was, he told me I'd know it if I saw it. I have a feeling he was taking the piss.

'Democritus believes that everything that exists is made up of tiny, tiny particles, which you can't actually see. He calls them "atoms," which means literally "things that can't be cut up." Well, if you can't see them, how can you possibly know they exist? You have to keep your wits about you when you're philosophising; that goes without saying.

'Today, of course, it's Socrates who's pulling in the crowds. I'm sure you've seen him. He's that short, fat geezer with a huge head and thick rubbery lips. Well, he doesn't actually pull in the crowds. He mainly hangs about with aristocrats. He despises common people. I tried to engage him in conversation once. He was in the Agora as usual, talking to a group of fawning toadies. "Hello, Socrates," I said good-naturedly, "I was hoping I'd bump into you one of these days. There's no one I've been more eager to meet. I wonder if you could define piety for me. I wish to point out that I'm something of a philosopher myself, so you won't need to talk down to me."

'Socrates responded by asking me what I thought piety was; as if I were the world's greatest expert on the subject. To cut a long story short, I proposed several very reasonable definitions, all of which Socrates poo-pooed. In the end I felt completely humiliated. If that was an example of his famous Socratic method in action, he can stuff it up his you-know-where. It's a useless way to teach. It merely exasperates the interlocutor. Added to which, I was no wiser at the end of our discussion than I had been at the beginning. No wonder so many Athenians can't stand him. He's an insufferable prig who pretends to be interested in what people say but who likes nothing better than to tie them in knots. He's doing a great disservice to philosophy by making it unpalatable to the masses.

'I've started hanging out in the Agora recently myself and sometimes a few people gather around to hear what I have to say. I tell them that existence is merely an illusion, that everything is nothing, and that we should all pool our resources together and live in a commune where the cult leader – that would be me – can sleep with any of his followers he likes. If you join my cult and follow some very basic rules, you will have the opportunity to come back in the next life as a cult leader in turn. That's a pretty good deal, no?

Sosippe, a Milesian call girl

'The first thing I want to make clear is that I'm certainly not a *pornê*, a prostitute, and I wouldn't be seen dead in a brothel. I'm a *hetaira*, "a companion". That's not to say I wouldn't engage in a bit of slap and tickle if the price is right, but that's not why I'm hired. I'm hired for my companionship, my skill in conversation, my good looks, and my wit.

'I was born and raised in Miletus, a city famous for its *hetairai*. I know how to converse intelligently about any subject under the sun: politics, literature, art, the gods, you name it. I can even give philosophers a run for their money when it comes to talking about what the universe is made of. I also play the flute and dance in a way that will excite any man. That's why I earn so much money.

'*Hetairai* are the only type of Greek women who are educated. The downside is that you've got to cut yourself off from your family and you obviously can't marry. You can, however, cohabit. Aspasia, who's also Milesian, cohabited with Pericles. He respected her so much that he often sought her advice before speaking in the Assembly.

'A lot of women look down their noses at *hetairai* because they see them as a threat to their identity. In my view that's just plain jealousy. Who wants to be stuck in the house all day long waiting to be told what to do by a man who's old enough to be your father? There's got to be more to life than that, and there jolly well is, let me assure you. I don't have any regrets for the life I've chosen to lead.

'Here's how I became a *hetaira*. My parents tried to marry me off to some filthy rich farmer called Ctesiphon, who lived in the back of beyond. I wasn't going to have any of it. So the week before the wedding I ran away. Ctesiphon had lost his wife a year previously. Well, "lost" is perhaps being rather generous. I wouldn't be surprised if he hadn't had something to do with her death. He was a brute of a man, quite capable of laying into a woman. He already had three children, aged two, four and five, so you can imagine what sort of life I would have been condemned to. Stuck indoors with a bunch of squawking kids and only a slave to keep me company. No, thank you!

'I ran to the nearest port and found a merchant who was sailing to Athens that same day. I was a virgin, so he readily agreed to take me on board on condition he could have his way with me. He treated me with respect and gave me a drachma for my services. The loss of my virginity was a small price to pay to escape a life of servitude to a man who would have treated me like dirt.

'When we docked in the Piraeus, I managed to hook up with some other Milesian women. They were only too willing to give me a leg up, so to speak, and they taught me the ropes.

'How I get hired is like this. Someone plans a symposium at his house. Maybe it's his birthday or he's won a competition or his wife's given birth, or maybe it's just a plain old drinking party. If a *hetaira* has any sense, she'll find out beforehand exactly what's expected of her. Sometimes sex is part of the deal, sometimes not. I allow petting but I draw the line at anything more than that these days, as I've moved up in the world.

'I've met some very interesting men in my time. I've knocked around with politicians, writers, sculptors, and, of course, philosophers. Philosophers are the worst, by the way. They can't keep their dirty paws off you. Last month I was invited to a symposium at the house of Agathon, the tragic poet who won the prize at the recent festival of Dionysus. Socrates was one of the guests. I have to say, he looked a total wreck. His cloak was filthy and his hair dishevelled. He also stank to high Olympus. I didn't let his appearance put me off, however. I was looking forward to hearing what he had to say for himself.

'First the guests appointed a symposiarch; that's the title of the person who's in charge of the proceedings. It's his task to direct things and make sure that everyone has a good time. I was expecting he'd liven things up by ordering the symposiasts to play a game that tests their knowledge of poetry. That always acts as an ice-breaker.

'Instead he suggested that they should give speeches about love. Everyone agreed, so I and the other *hetairai* were told to leave. I thought this was pretty naff, but we'd been paid for our services in advance, so it was no skin off our noses.

'The girls and I managed to crash another symposium where our talents were very much appreciated. I have to confess I got a bit drunk and let the man reclining next to me get more than he should have. We continued drinking till dawn and he gave me a generous tip when we parted, so it was all in a good cause, so to speak.

'I can't help wondering what Socrates had to say about love. What in the name of all the gods does that broken down old fart know about it? He must be at least sixty if he's a day. He looked as if he hadn't dipped his wick in a month of public holidays.

Makareus, a blind beggar

'I wasn't born a beggar. No one ever is, of course. I wasn't born blind either. I used to live on the east coast of Attica, in the deme of Thorikos. My parents both died in a fire when I was seven and my aunt Hedylla brought me up. I'd inherited a small patch of land on a slope within sight of the sea that is only good for growing olives. I couldn't afford a slave, so I had to do all the work myself. My uncle taught me the ropes, but when he died I was left on my own.

'When the war broke out, I moved to the city and when I returned I discovered all my trees had been cut down. It takes about fifteen years for an olive tree to start producing olives and at least forty before it reaches maturity. I was ruined, in other words. I had no alternative but to sell up.

'I didn't get much for my farm and what I did get I soon squandered. I couldn't adjust to life in the city. There were too many distractions and too many temptations for a young man like myself. After a year or two I decided to offer my services as a prostitute. I did well to begin with on account of my good looks. But then I caught the disease and my skin became riddled with sores. I also went blind in one eye.

'I moved down to the Piraeus and managed to eke out a modest living from sailors, but eventually that source of income dried up. I wasn't sorry to call it a day. I'd had some pretty unsavoury customers in my time. All sorts of people live in the Piraeus; non-Greeks as well as Greeks. The worst are the Egyptians. Once they get into their cups [drunk], there's nothing they won't ask you to do. And they're stingy as well.

'After that, I began working as a labourer. A vase painter called Onesimos hired me for an obol a day to do work any slave could have done: washing his brushes, keeping the kiln at the right temperature, and cleaning up after him. After three or four months, however, I began to lose the sight of my other eye and I started stumbling into things. One day I smashed a vase which Onesimos had been working on for a wealthy client and he threw me out. I could hardly blame him. I'd become a liability.

'So that, in a nutshell, is how I became a beggar. I'd only the cloak on my back at this point to call my own, so I was living from hand to mouth. Being a beggar isn't easy. You have to fight for your turf. Eventually I managed to nab a spot at the entrance to the agora in the Piraeus. I may be blind, but I'm still strong and I've been able to see off many another beggar who has tried to steal my spot. Remember how in the *Odyssey* Odysseus, disguised as a beggar, gets into a fight with Irus, the beggar who has taken up occupancy in his palace?

'Every morning I pray to a little statue of Ptocheia, the goddess who protects beggars, which I fashioned out of clay. Well, Ptocheia isn't exactly a goddess. She's just a humble *daimôn*, a divine spirit. But she protects me all the same. I know that she's looking after me because last month a cripple who was muscling in on my patch got crushed by a fully-laden cart. The cart missed me by a hair's breadth.

144

'I'm fortunate to have a woman who looks after me. Her name is Clio; same name as the famed muse of history. She brings me scraps of food and a pitcher of wine every evening. Sometimes she stays and then we bed down together under a blanket. I'm lucky to have the use of all my fingers. The sickness didn't rob me of those, as it did most poor sods, thank the gods. The rest, in a manner of speaking, is history.

Bion, an enslaved merchant from Ephesus

'I had the bad luck to be captured by pirates on my first voyage abroad with my father. After sailing from Ephesus, we'd docked at the island of Samos, where we picked up a hundred amphorae of wine. Samian wine, as you probably know, is the best. We sold it for a good price in Syracuse and were on our way back home, hugging the coast as per normal.

'After we set sail from Corcyra [modern-day Corfu], however, a pirate ship came alongside us. We didn't stand a chance. There were a couple of Athenian triremes in the harbour – Athens is an ally of Corcyra – but they didn't do anything to protect us.

'The pirates boarded our vessel, threw us in irons, and sailed to Epirus on the west coast of Greece, where there's a large slave market. As soon as we disembarked, I was separated from my father and I've never set eyes on him since. Who knows where he has ended up? As for my mother, I think of her sitting at home, growing increasingly anxious at the long delay, first hoping against hope that one day we will walk in the door, and then eventually accepting the fact that she will never see either of us again.

'There were thousands of slaves being auctioned, divided up according to sex, age, looks, education, ethnicity, and so forth. I'm literate and fairly presentable, so I was herded into a pen with others like me who were expected to fetch a pretty good price. I remember an attractive Thracian girl who went for 165 drachmas and a Carian boy for 174. Bear in mind that the usual daily wage is about one drachma per day – just enough to support a family – so many of the bidders were extremely wealthy.

'I was made to strip, handed a loincloth to cover my private parts, and told to stand in a long line awaiting my turn. Several potential buyers inspected me, prodding me, examining my teeth, stroking my leg, you name it. The youth in front of me was an Egyptian. Egyptians are especially prized because they're circumcised, a practice that Greeks find exotic.

'Eventually it was my turn to be auctioned. I was directed to mount a platform and ordered to remove my loincloth. I had to turn around slowly with my arms outstretched. You can imagine how humiliating this was. Only a few days ago, I'd been a free man. Now I was no more than an object.

'The bidding proceeded rapidly. Eventually, a Corinthian called Aphareus bought me for 240 drachmas. I was one of eight slaves he acquired that day.

'It took us nearly a month to reach Corinth. We got caught in a squall and had to land in Acarnania, the region on the west coast just north of the Peloponnese. We remained in Acarnania several days, doing repairs to the hull and mending the sails. We passed through the Gulf of Corinth and then our boat was hauled across the isthmus along the paved track known as the *Diolkos*. The shorter days were coming on when we finally reached the port of Lechaion.

'Aphareus lived in a large house not far from the port. He was married and had one son aged sixteen, a spoilt brat called Thibrakos. He'd had a distinguished career as a Corinthian general. He was a good man. He never beat me and he never overworked me. I got decent food and was allowed to sleep in the house. His wife was ok too. She left me pretty much alone, which was all I could have asked.

'Most of the work Aphareus asked me to do was of a scribal nature. He was writing a history of Corinth and would dictate to me every day for hours. Sometimes he would nod off in mid-sentence and I'd sit quietly waiting for him to wake up, which he generally did with a jolt. Then he'd carry on as if nothing had happened.

'One afternoon, however, he nodded off and didn't wake up. I called my mistress – I didn't dare touch him – and she started screaming and then all the other slaves came rushing in. His death moved me. He used to say that if the gods had ordered things differently, I would be dictating to him and that everything comes down to fortune in the end.

'After he died, my life changed for the worse. His widow fell sick and hardly ever got off her couch and Thibrakos began running things. He had no time for literature, so he got me working in the fields, doing the worst jobs he could find, as if to punish me for having been favoured by his father. I was banished to one of the outhouses and all my privileges were removed. I even had to sleep in a leg iron at night.

'While working in the fields some distance from the house, I decided to take my chances and ran off. Thibrakos set the dogs after me but I threw them off by wading into a river. I lay low for a few days and then headed to Lechaion. I had stolen some of my mistress' jewellery and bought a *chitôn* so that I could present myself as a respectable freeborn citizen in the hope to getting a place on board a ship back to Ephesus, though who knows what I'll find back home.'

Memnon, a Spartan hoplite

'I can't imagine anything more honourable than being a Spartan soldier. The state is everything. I'd die in a heartbeat for it. In our entire history we've never lost a single battle. The battle of Thermopylae wasn't a defeat. It was a victory. Every one of the 300 stood his ground. And don't forget we were fighting against the entire Persian army, over a million men in all. Xerxes sent a spy to see what the 300 were doing before the battle. He reported that they were combing their hair. That's what we always do before we put ourselves in harm's way. That rattled the Persians for sure. They quickly realised they were up against the greatest fighting machine the world had ever seen.

'"Go tell the Spartans, you who pass by, that here obedient to their laws we lie," is the famous epigram that the poet Simonides wrote on behalf of the 300. No claim for sympathy, far less any attempt at self-glorification. Very laconic, in other words. That's the Spartans for you.

'The Athenians are always calling us stupid and ignorant. But would you want to live in that city of chatterboxes, everyone arguing all the time, everybody taking everybody to court? It must be a dreadful place. Spartans don't go around making long speeches all the time. They just get on with the job. If you ask an Athenian what he wants, he won't give you a straight answer. He'll ask you what you mean by "want" and then he'll proceed to chew your ear off. Athenians mock us because we get to the point immediately.

'They also mock us for the fact that only a few of us can read or write. But what fun is there in reading or writing in a room by yourself, when you could be exchanging stories about Spartan valour in the company of

147

your mates? Yes, it's true that the Athenians enjoy more leisure than we do, but frankly I think leisure is overrated.

'There's a lull in the hostilities between us and the Athenians at the moment, but it's only temporary and we'll beat them in the end, no question. Our victory at Thermopylae made us the most feared soldiers in the whole world. The amazing thing is that our fighting strength is actually quite small; just a few thousand men in total. The biggest problem we're facing is that we're not producing enough babies. The number of Spartiates has even begun to decrease. We've a law that if a husband doesn't succeed in impregnating his wife, he has to let someone else have a go. Let's hope that solves the declining birth rate. I'm certainly up for the challenge!'

Gnotho, a helot

'Let me be clear from the start: helots aren't slaves. We're a conquered people. There's a big difference. Elsewhere in the Greek world slaves lack any ethnic identity. They don't have their own traditions, their own gods, or their own history. They don't live in families either.

'But helots are a race apart. The Spartans conquered our homeland centuries ago, but we've never forgotten that we were once a free people. And one day we'll be free again. That's why they fear us so much. They know we're powerful. Whenever they go off on campaign, they're always looking over their shoulders, wondering what we're up to, and they hurry back as soon as they can to make sure we aren't plotting against them. Imagine that. The so-called greatest fighting machine that the world has ever seen, terrified of a bunch of unarmed men!

'Well, they've got every reason to be afraid of us. We don't live in Laconia. That's the territory that the Spartans occupy. We live in Messenia, our land to the west. To get to Messenia from Laconia, you have to cross a range of mountains. About two generations ago, in the year of the Great Earthquake, our forefathers revolted. Several thousand of them took refuge on Ithome, our sacred mountain.

'Our forefathers nearly brought the Spartans to their knees. The Athenians offered to help crush the revolt, but the Spartans turned them down because they didn't trust them. The Athenians had recently introduced big democratic changes and the Council of Elders was afraid that the same changes might catch on in Sparta.

148

'Eventually the revolt was crushed, but the memory of those heroic times remains very much alive. We tell the story to our children, and they'll tell it to their children, and one day we'll rise up again and kill all the Spartans in their beds.

'Most helots are farmers. We cultivate the land – our land – for the Spartans, who act as absentee landowners. They barely allow us enough food to support our families, but at least they leave us alone to get on with our lives. However, they're paranoid about what we might be getting up to, so every year they formally declare war against us. They don't actually send an army into Messenia. Instead the so-called war is a way of training Spartan youths before they become hoplites. They call serving in this war the *krupteia*, which means close to 'secret police'. The youths live in the wild and attack us without warning.

'They sleep rough for a couple of years, either singly or in small groups. They can steal our belongings, burn down our houses, rape our women, or abduct our children. It's open season against all helots. They never get punished for their crimes because they don't see their behaviour as criminal. The whole point of the exercise is to terrorise us so that we don't do anything "stupid".

'There's nothing more terrifying than a raid by members of the *krupteia*. They generally attack in the middle of the night. They don't wear armour and they have to make their own weapons, so sometimes we're able to repulse them. If we do, the chances are that they'll be back again the next night, and the next night, till they've done what they intend to do. It's all random. You never know when you might face an attack. My parents died at their hands when I was about fifteen years old.

'A year or so after their death I caught sight of a Spartan youth hunting. After checking to make sure he was unaccompanied, I picked up a heavy rock and struck him in the thigh. I could have killed him outright but I was thinking about what had happened to my parents and I wanted him to die a slow and painful death. He was crying like a newborn. That's the best sight in the world, to see a Spartan fearing for his life. I lifted up another rock and crushed his leg so that he couldn't even crawl any more. Then I fetched a bowl of water and left it just out of his range. When I returned three days later, the dogs and the vultures had had their way with him.

'Not all helots live in Messenia. A few trusted ones are assigned to Spartan families as domestics. An even smaller number are trained to fight. What gets conveniently overlooked about the 300 who fought at Thermopylae is that there was an army of helots fighting there too, and that if it hadn't been for them, the 300 would have been wiped out on the first day. After the battle, the Spartan propaganda machine worked overtime to cast it as a purely Spartan victory. Our contribution was completely forgotten.

'We're a very special people and we bring up our children to be very proud of their ancestry. Just don't make the mistake of calling us slaves.'

Glossary

Acropolis – Literally 'high part of the city'; a defensible rock on which many of the most venerable cults are located. Though almost every *polis* has an acropolis, the most famous acropolis is that of Athens.

agora – A level space in the centre of a Greek town that functions as its civic, commercial, legal, and political heart.

andrôn – A room in the house designated for the holding of a symposium (literally 'men's quarters').

Archaic – The period of Greek history conventionally dated c.630-480.

archon – Literally 'leader'; one of nine senior magistrates in Classical Athens appointed by lot, the most important being the eponymous archon, who gives his name to the year.

Assembly – Together with the Council, the Assembly comprises one of the two primary organs of Greek governance.

Attica – The entire territory of the Athenian state.

Ceramicus – Literally 'potters' quarter', a burial area outside the city walls of Athens on the west side.

chitôn – An ankle-length garment worn by both men and women.

City Dionysia – The festival held in honour of Dionysus, at which both tragedies and comedies are performed.

Classical – The term used to describe the period of Greek history dated 480-323. The Classical period begins with the battle of Marathon and ends with the death of Alexander the Great.

deme – One of about 150 townships into which Attica is divided.

Demos Name for the citizen body as a whole, i.e. the People.

drachma – A silver coin equivalent to a day's pay in the late-fifth century.

ephebe – Literally 'one who is at the prime of life'; a term used of an Athenian youth, who, having reached his eighteenth year, is undergoing a two-year stint of military training.

genos – Noble kin-group.

Great Dionysia – The Athenian festival in honour of Dionysus, at which plays are performed.

gymnasium – Literally 'a place of nakedness'; a training establishment where men exercise and converse together.

gynaikônitis – The women's quarters of a house.

helots – A term of uncertain etymology used to describe the enslaved inhabitants of Messenia who work for the Spartans.

herm – An image of the god Hermes, consisting of carved head and genitals, set on a pillar that marks the boundaries of a property.

hetaira – Literally a 'female companion'; a woman who is paid for her companionship, including, but not exclusively, her sexual favours.

himation – A woollen cloak worn by both men and women.

Hippocrates – The legendary founder of rational medicine and author of the so-called Hippocratic oath.

hoplite – Heavily-armed Greek infantryman, named for his circular bronze shield or *hoplon*.

Ionia – The term used by the Greeks to identify the central western coast of modern-day Turkey and its offshore islands.

Laconia – The territory occupied by the Spartans.

Macedon, Macedonia – The kingdom that lies between the Balkans and the southern peninsula of mainland Greece.

Messenia – The territory to the west of Sparta, occupied by the helots.

metic – Literally 'a person who has changed his *oikos*,' i.e. a legal resident alien.

miasma – Ritual pollution caused primarily by the shedding of blood and by death.

oikia, oikos – A household or family, comprising not only family members but also buildings, property, slaves and animals.

paidagôgos – A slave who accompanies his master's son outside the home and is responsible for his welfare.

Panathenaea – The Athenian festival held in honour of Athena's birthday.

panhellenic – Literally 'all-Greek'; the term refers to events and institutions in which all Greek speakers are free to participate.

Peloponnese – Literally 'the island of Pelops'; the term used to denote the part of mainland Greece that lies south of the isthmus of Corinth.

peplos – An ankle-length woollen garment worn by girls and women.

phalanx – The principal hoplite formation, usually eight rows deep.

polis – Conventionally rendered 'city state', the term describes an autonomous political entity consisting of an urban centre and surrounding territory.

sophist – An itinerant teacher of rhetoric.

stoa – A colonnaded building, which serves many purposes and provides shelter from the elements.

symposium – Literally a 'drinking together,' attended exclusively by men and *hetairai*.

trireme – A modern term for a Greek warship with three banks of oars.

Credits

Author: 11, 14, 19, 20, 21, 24, 25, 39, 40
Andy Daddio: 16, 17
Michael Holobosky: 1, 2, 3, 4
Shutterstock: 5, 6, 7, 8, 9, 10, 12, 13, 15, 18, 22, 23, 26, 27, 28, 29, 30, 31, 32, 33, 34, 35, 36, 37, 38